PARADISE FOUND

THE SETTLEMENT OF THE SANTA CATALINA MOUNTAINS

By Kathy Alexander

Published by Skunkworks Productions,
Mt. Lemmon, Arizona 85619
Maps by Paul Lindsey
Cover Illustration by Armand Baltazar
Library of Congress 91-060151
ISBN 0-962-8832-0-4

Second printing

Printed on Recycled Paper

From every street and corner in Tucson we see the mountains. From our places of business, from our railway depots and hotels, from our University campus and halls, and from the windows and porches of our homes we look up to the mighty hills.

But of all the peaks and ranges that keep their sentinel posts around this old pueblo, there are none so bold in outlines of their granite heights and rugged canons, so exquisitely beautiful in their soft colors of red and purple, or so luring in their call of the remote and hidden fastnesses as the Santa Catalinas...Even in the darkness we see their shadowy might against the sky and feel the still and solemn mystery of their enduring strength under the desert stars.

Harold Bell Wright
The Mine with the Iron Door
1923

This book is dedicated to Tony Zimmerman--a man
who loved the Catalinas with all his heart.

The author thanks Paul Lindsey and Ted Knipe for their support
and assistance during the preparation of this book.

PREFACE

On a beautiful autumn day in 1988, my husband and I left our Mt. Lemmon cabin to hike in the aspens. When we returned, we were horrified to discover that our cabin had burned to the ground during our brief absence. The fire deeply saddened us, in part because we had lost our vacation home, but also because an old cabin, which typified what life must have been like on Mt. Lemmon many years ago, had been destroyed.

According to long-time Mt. Lemmon resident Tony Zimmerman our cabin had been built in the 1930's by a prospector named Grady who was looking for gold. Because of the cabin's difficult site, mules were used to bring down the lumber from the sawmill and the tin for the roof. Old Grady had done a pretty good job--the walls were relatively straight, the roof did not leak, and the cabin had stood at its precarious location hanging off the side of a very steep hill for more than 50 years. He had obviously appreciated the dramatic scenery as he had placed the outhouse so that its occupant had a magnificent view of the valley and mountains beyond. Grady eventually got in a jam as he tried to sell some mining claims he did not own, and fled to Mexico, abandoning his little house.

During my many blissful days and nights in that old cabin, I wondered about the history of the Santa Catalina Mountains and people like Grady. As I sat on our rickety porch during those summer afternoon rains, watching the fog roll down the valley, I could almost feel the presence of those from long ago who had loved these mountains as much as I do.

I have written this brief book for those of you who really know and care about the Catalinas and want to learn about what has happened here before.

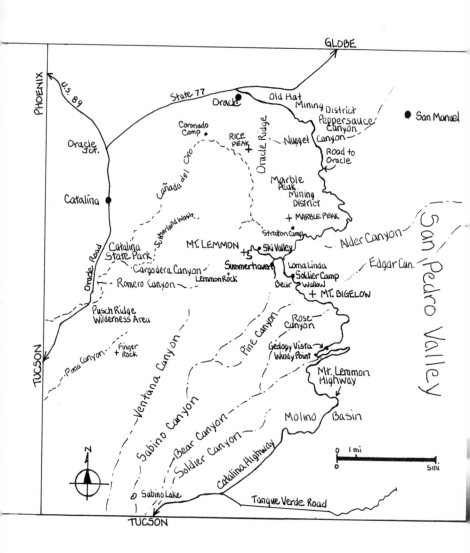

MAP 1 - PLACE NAMES IN THE SANTA CATALINAS

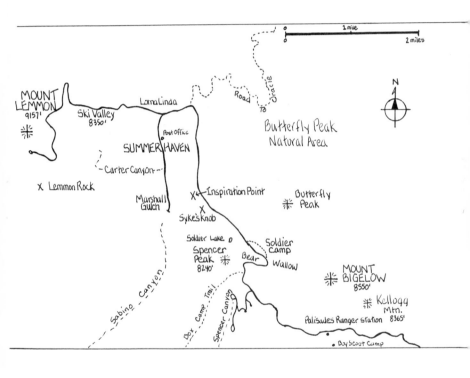

MAP 2 - PLACE NAMES IN THE SUMMERHAVEN AND SOLDIER CAMP AREAS

TABLE OF CONTENTS

Chapter One

THE ASCENT BEGINS

The Catalina Highway twists and turns around dozens of hairpin curves climbing nearly 6500 feet in 25 miles. The dramatic climate changes from the desert valley to the peaks of the Catalinas have attracted people to these mountains for centuries. The Santa Catalina Mountains are sometimes called "desert sky islands" which is a term used to describe nearly a dozen mountain ranges in southeastern Arizona that rise from the desert floor and have a natural environment at the peak drastically different from that of the surrounding desert. Several natural life zones are experienced during the drive up the Catalina Highway. In fact, it is said that the 25 mile trip to the top of the mountains is like driving from Mexico to Canada, in terms of the life zones that are encountered. At the bottom, the terrain is Lower Sonoran Desert, with many saguaro and other cacti, trees and shrubs. The area at the top (elevation 9157') is a mixed conifer Canadian zone, with Douglas fir, aspen, ponderosa pine, gambel's oak, locust and bracker fern. For hundreds of summers, this area has provided a haven for desert dwellers who wish to cool off in temperatures about 25 degrees lower than those on the desert floor. This is the story of the people who have sought refuge here from the heat, aridity and pressures of daily living in the surrounding region.

Some of the earliest human inhabitants to enjoy this climate were the Hohokam who lived in these mountains as far back as 100 B.C.. Remains of their villages and rock art are found throughout the lower elevations of the Catalinas and at a few places near the peaks. The Hohokam lived in pit houses and sustained themselves by growing corn and gathering wild beans and fruits and some hunting. Most of the Hohokam pictographs are found northeast of Catalina State Park near Sutherland Wash. Hohokam art is also found in Sabino Canyon and near La Milagosa Falls. In some of these sites, other remnants of the Hohokam culture have been located, including pottery shards, flaked and ground stones, bedrock mortars and possibly refuse piles and home sites. The Hohokam rock art in the Catalinas is extensive, located at 14 sites with over 1400 drawings. These pictures include images of humans as well as birds and bird tracks, lizards, toads, snakes, bear paws and sheep, plus more abstract drawings of circles, wavy lines and spirals. The original purpose of this art is not known, although it is conjectured that the art may have marked trails or sacred sites or simply served as decoration.[1] The Hohokam disappeared around 1400 A.D..

Sometime after the Hohokam's departure, the Arivaipa Apaches made the north side of the Santa Catalina Mountains their summer home. This Apache band's territory included the San Pedro Valley from about 20 miles north of present day Benson to the Globe/Miami area. Their territory also included part of the Galiuro Mountains. The northern slopes of the Catalinas provided good hunting and concealment from other native people and settlers.[2]

The exact sites in the Catalinas where the Apaches lived are impossible to determine because the Apaches, unlike many current visitors, left little trash or other remains of their culture. Some Apache rock art remains in Edgar Canyon near Pictograph Spring. At this site, fifteen pictographs are found on a boulder sheltered by an overhang, including the depiction of two black turtle-like creatures and a large buff-colored eagle. Other art exists at the site which was not done by the Apaches and was probably crafted by Indians who preceded the Apaches. Since the Apaches revered the rock art of their predecessors, they typically selected these same sites to add their own motifs.[3]

Although there is no documented description of specific Apache settlements in the Catalinas, it is easy to guess what they may have been like from the records of Apache settlements in other southeastern Arizona mountains. Apaches were nomadic and constructed their homes, called wickiups, in about four hours, using materials abundant in these mountains. The Apache women built the wickiups from a framework of poles and limbs covered with grass, brush, bark and/or deerskins. Sometimes canvas was thrown over the wickiups for wind protection. After the main frame was completed, dirt from the center of the floor was scooped out and piled around the base of the interior of the wickiup, which helped protect the occupants from cold and rain and solidified the structure. In cold weather, the Apaches built a small fire in the center, allowing the smoke to escape from a hole they left in the roof. In the summer, the Apaches sometimes abandoned the wickiups and constructed ramadas of poles and brush to provide needed shade.

When the Apaches lived in the Catalinas, the wildlife was somewhat more varied than today. Today, the casual visitor to the Catalinas rarely sees more than an assortment of birds and a number of chipmunks and squirrels, with an occasional raccoon and spotted skunk. But at the time of the Apache settlements, black bears, antelope, deer, elk, wolves, jaguar, fox and wild turkeys were scattered throughout the range and there may have been grizzlies in the area as well. Several herds of big horn sheep roamed the mountains at mid elevations.[4]

TYPICAL APACHE WICKIUPS AND A RAMADA - PERHAPS LIKE THOSE FOUND IN THE SANTA CATALINA MOUNTAINS. (Courtesy of the Arizona Historical Society, Tucson, Arizona, #50814)

These animals provided the Indians with many of the supplies they needed. Although they would not eat bear due to religious objections, they could find other meat, such as deer, which they fried, broiled, jerked or boiled. Additional staples found in the mountains included agave, walnuts, juniper berries, acorns and the inner bark of the Ponderosa pine. The acorns, called bellotas, were a favorite food and were most often taken from the Emory oak. The northern foothills of the Catalinas was a favorite spot of the Apaches for acorn gathering.[5] Most of their clothing was made of buckskin, the source of which was readily available in the mountains. The mountains also provided the Texas mulberry, which was a choice wood for making bows.

The Apaches were distressed, to say the least, by the arrival of the Spanish in the Santa Cruz valley in the late 17th century. From the valley, the Spanish deeply admired the Catalinas and called them "La Iglesia," which means the church. This name

4

was given because they thought that the view of the mountains from Tucson resembled a great cathedral.

Although the evidence is weak, it is widely believed that Father Eusebio Kino renamed the mountains in 1697. According to this legend, Kino called them the Santa Catarina Mountains, which was the name used until the spelling was changed to the Santa Catalina Mountains in the 1880's. Some say that Father Kino may have visited or seen the region on Saint Catherine's day and named them after the saint, which was a common practice. Others believe he named the mountains after his sister. There is evidence that a Jesuit mission was located near the northern foothills of the Catalina Mountains in the Canada del Oro area in the 1690's. This parish was called Santa Catalina de Cuitabagu, which means "well where people gather mesquite beans." It was later moved to a site near current downtown Tucson. The site of the original mission cannot now be located.[6] The mountains may have been named after the mission or the mission named after the mountains.

The clashes between the Spanish and the Apaches are well known. Throughout the 1700's and through most of the 1800's, Apaches raided the Santa Cruz valley, killing settlers and taking livestock. Some of these raids may have been made by the Arivaipa band who sometimes resided in the Catalinas, although some experts believe that this group was the least warlike of all the Apaches. The Catalina Mountains were a great refuge for the Apaches after their attacks, and the Spanish military forces frequently searched the Catalinas looking for the offending Indians. In 1779, Captain Pedro de Allande, Spanish Commandant of the newly formed Tucson presidio, made a campaign into the Catalinas where he attacked two Apache camps. He killed some warriors, women and children and took six prisoners. In June 1783, Allande led a force of 96 men into the Santa Catalinas where they killed two Apaches and wounded two others. He displayed the Apaches' heads in Tucson. In

5

1785, he campaigned through the Catalinas and other mountains, burning Apache settlements and killing any warriors he could find. After a raid by Apaches in 1794, a group of 44 soldiers and five civilians, battled and defeated the Indians a few miles north of Tucson. They later discovered that an additional group of nearly a hundred Apache warriors had been in the Santa Catalinas ready to ambush them had they been drawn into the trap by the raiders.[7]

In spite of the presence of the Apaches, Tucson was beginning to be an important hub of transportation in southern Arizona by the mid 1800's. The major supply route north from Tucson to Ft. Grant passed through the Canada del Oro area in the western foothills of the Catalinas. Many skirmishes with the Apaches occurred in this area, as the Apaches could spot travellers down on the road from a lookout point in the mountains and then retreat back into the Catalinas after an attack. A typical raid occurred in May, 1869, when Apaches struck the wagon trains of Tully and Ochoa at Canada del Oro. The drivers managed to escape, but all goods and equipment were lost.[8] In March 1872, an U.S. Army Paymaster camped in the Canada del Oro area after leaving Camp Grant on his way to Tucson. He camped on a "high spur" of the mountains opposite a high peak covered with pines and snow and noted that:

> Our road today has many graves along the way and wrecks of trains. It is in a part of the country where the Apaches acknowledge no authority but their own, and their bands are against every traveler and every train. We passed a very uncomfortable night on our high perch; I had a presentiment of Indians, which rather interfered with sleeping.[9]

Some nicknamed this stretch of road "The Graveyard." If at all possible, travel in this area was done only with a military escort.

6

Camp Lowell had been established in 1866 near present day downtown Tucson to help protect the settlers against the Apaches. In 1873, Camp Lowell was renamed Fort Lowell and moved to a site along the Rillito about six miles to the north. Some of the logs were brought from the Catalina pine forests to construct the roofs of the fort's buildings. The military reservation of the Fort bordered the Santa Catalina Mountains on the north. The soldiers, no doubt, visited these mountains until 1891 when the fort was abandoned. It is believed that Soldier Camp (currently a picnic and summer home area) was a place frequented by the soldiers, although the Ft. Lowell military records do not document this. The soldiers' love of hunting is known, and it seems quite likely that they would have followed Sabino Canyon up into the mountains which would have taken them near the present day Soldier Camp. The soldiers' legacy to these mountains is recorded in several place names including Soldier Camp, Canyon and Trail. One Indian fighter whose name is remembered in the Catalinas spent little, if any, time there. Lt. John Bigelow, Jr. was a scout in the Santa Rita and the Graham mountains. One of the highest peaks in the Catalinas bears his name.

In 1874, Chunz, a renegade Apache leader who was wanted desperately by the U. S. Army, was found to be hiding in the "precipices of the Santa Caterrina" Mountains. He had been tracked there by an Apache who had surrendered to the U. S. Army and had been ordered to find Chunz and bring in his head. The fight in the Catalinas lasted a day during which several of Chunz's party were wounded and surrendered. Chunz managed to escape from the Catalinas, but was killed and beheaded a few days later.[10]

The Apaches were officially subdued in 1885. However, reports of trouble with the Apaches continued intermittently during the next several years. In early June, 1887, seventeen Apache Indians took refuge on the north side of the Catalinas.[11] Later that same time, Tucsonans believed that the Apaches had set fires in the Catalinas and it was feared that 25,000 acres of timber would be destroyed.[12] Although the Apache Wars were supposedly over, these incidents must have made the soldiers at the Fort a little wary. Perhaps that is why they scouted through the Catalinas for nine days in 1888. They covered almost the entire length of the main ridge which was a distance of 95 miles, but made no reports of Apache activities.[13] Although in 1890, the Arizona Daily Star mentioned that about 20 Apaches had been seen at Sabino Canyon and that two Apache Indians had shot at two Mexican boys at the San Miguel mine in the Catalina Mountains, the Apaches exclusive use of the Catalinas had come to an end.[14]

Chapter Two

HIDDEN TREASURES

Many mountains inspire tales of lost treasures and the Catalinas are no exception. According to one legend, the Jesuit missionaries buried gold and silver in the Santa Catalinas in the "Mine with the Iron Door" during an Indian uprising in 1751. This mine was believed to be on the west side of the mountains in the Canada del Oro area. This story first appeared in the Tucson newspapers in the 1880's.[15] Although the Pima Indians did revolt against the Spanish in 1751, the rest of the story has never been documented. Another legend holds that Indians buried a treasure in the Catalinas somewhere along an imaginary line stretching from San Xavier del Bac several miles south of Tucson to La Ventanita (the Window) in Ventana Canyon. This treasure, too, has remained safe from discovery.

Mining in the Catalinas began before the Apaches had been subdued, when many daring Arizonans were caught up in the gold and silver frenzy occurring throughout the West. Prospectors were investigating every rocky ridge, and the Santa Catalinas had plenty. For the first time, mountains such as the

Catalinas began to be viewed as valuable resources, instead of simply obstacles for travelers or a refuge for Apache raiders.

One of the earliest detailed records of the exploration of these mountains comes from Issac Goldberg and his party of 11 explorers and prospectors who searched for gold in the Catalinas in 1871. They did not find the easy riches they had sought--an experience that was repeated by many others. The following are excerpts from Goldberg's recollections of this unfruitful trip:

> Much disappointed we stood and gazed at the vast area of country which lay far below, and resolved an immediate return to Tucson. I asked the guide how many days would probably be consumed in journeying and he answered "two", but no less than eight days had expired ere we reached our goal.

> Almost incredible hardships attended and encumbered our progress homeward---narrow steep trails, between dreadful abysses, exhausting tracts of rocky sterility, and patches of brush so thick and thorny that our wary bodies lost their coverings and our blistered feet their leather protectors. We were nearly naked, barefoot, and on the very brink of starvation, for we had no food during this dangerous expedition, except for a small quantity of pinole and some wild grapes. I found a mine, the rocks from which assayed richly, but the contents yet remain undisturbed, owing to its uncommon inaccessibility, We had, however, attained the distinction of being the first explorers of the terrible precipitous heights known as the Santa Catalina Mountains.[16]

In 1878, Martinique native Issac Lorraine, established a successful lead and silver mine on the north side of the Santa Catalinas, which he called the American Flag, and soon gold prospecting and mining were in full swing. The fervor of the local people regarding the potential of minerals in the area is summed up by the conclusion of an article in the local paper:

> There are few mining districts which present as many attractive features as the Santa Catalinas, or as great a diversity of minerals. Wood, water, and the prime necessities are abundant and easily obtained, and the would be investor, within a radius of a few miles, can have his choice of gold, silver, or copper properties.[17]

In the same year, a Scotsman, Alexander McKay, came to the north side of the Catalinas to work on Albert Weldon's mining claim "Oracle" which had been named after Weldon's uncle's ship. The town of Oracle was later named after the mine. McKay encountered isolation, with occasional contact from Indians in his first few months in the Catalinas:

> There was no house of any kind out there and I had to sleep under a fly (a cloth flap which forms a roof extension for a tent or wagon) One morning while I was baking bread in a Dutch oven I heard a whistle. It sounded weird as I thought I was miles away from everyone. Looking up, I saw an Indian coming toward me. He kept saying "Me George. Me Eskiminzin's man. More come. Eskiminzin come." After a while, sure enough, Eskiminzin and a band of Indians--men, women, and children--came along. They had two quarters of venison tied on their pack. They told me they wanted some flour. Well, I knew they would take the flour anyway, so I offered to trade for a quarter of venison, and they did. I was a little disconcerted when they camped right next to me and the next morning I did not go prospecting, but sat on the hill where I could watch camp all day. They did not disturb anything however but soon moved on. On Christmas day I located the Christmas mine and the next week another I called the New Year.

The next year I built the first house in Oracle, a one roomed adobe for me and Weldon. There was nothing going on in those days but Indian and game trails going in all directions...I have had as many as five deer hanging in a tree at one time...We had a pet bull snake at the mine which would follow me to water. But one day a visitor came in exclaiming, "My God boys. I just killed the biggest snake I ever saw right at the door."[18]

Two distinct mining districts began to develop along the Oracle Ridge, where nearly all of the mining in the Catalinas has occurred. One mining district, in the Marble Peak area, included the Geesaman, Leatherwood, Stratton, Daily, Control, Hartman and Battleship mines. About three miles north of this area, near Peppersauce Canyon, was another group of mines sometimes called the Old Hat district, that included the Apache Girl, Southern Belle, American Flag, Bonito, Old Maudina and the Hijinks mines.[19] A few mines were also located in the Canada del Oro area, which is not surprising since "oro" is the Spanish word for gold.

One of the best discoveries of gold in the Old Hat district was made in 1880 or 1881 by the wife of prospector Capt. John T. Young while she brought him his lunch. Ms. Young sat down on a ledge to rest and described how she made the discovery:

> Without thinking...I pulled out a hairpin and began picking at the whitish vein that meandered through the ledge. Something dull yellow was in the specimen I loosened...I gathered the specimens into my husband's handkerchief and hurried on to (my husband.) We both forgot the dinner and...rushed down the hill to the outcrop. With his pick, my husband pried off larger and larger specimens from what he called a blanket ledge... He seemed unable to believe my strike was...the richest gold ore he had ever

12

seen. He stuttered when he tried to show me the value of my discovery."[20]

Appropriately, the mine was named after Mrs. Young and was called the Southern Belle. Its yield was one of the richest in the area.

Supposedly, the largest nugget ever found in the Catalinas was found in what is now known as Nugget Canyon. Although the weight of the nugget is not known, it was so big that the lucky prospector who found it could barely lift it. In order to carry it back to his camp, he took off his pants and put the nugget in one leg and tied the leg shut with his belt.[21]

In 1881, an unnamed traveler explored the mining districts on the north side of the Catalinas and described his journey in great detail for those Tucsonans who would probably never have a chance to see the area for themselves. The following are excerpts from his description of the mining areas:

At Oracle Camp, the Old Hat mining district commences. The whole region hereabout as I verified by personal inspection, is seamed by promising quartz ledges...It is surprising that the district still remains so backward. The claim owners are, however, poor men who have done their development work as best they could and are praying for the advent of capital. Their hopes seem likely to be realized.

About two miles beyond Flag camp is Captain Young's ranch, the limit of stage travel and the head of prairie schooner navigation on this route. Here is situated the Imperial Mine, which of late has had a rather unfortunate experience, and has involved its owners..in considerable loss...An effort to mill the ore has proven disastrous, and the mill has been dismantled and the machinery taken

13

ONE OF THE WORKINGS OF THE STRATTON MINE NEAR MARBLE PEAK, 1900. (Courtesy of the Arizona Historical Society, Tucson, Arizona, #631)

away...Various reasons are ascribed for the failure, some assigning it to the inefficiency of the mill...and other to mismanagement.

About two miles from here and further up the canyon, Sam Parkenson keeps bachelor's hall in the Stone Cabin (near his Apache Girl mine)...About a mile from here, some Slavonians are developing a narrow but rich lode called the Gold Nugget.

The traveler then progresses to the mining area around Marble Peak:

An exceedingly eccentric trail leads from the spring to Stratton's...In company with Messrs. Stratton and Felter, the owners of the Comanche copper mine, I inspected...mines (that) are well up in the mountains, within a few hundred feet of the pine timber at the summit and at an altitude of 7,300 feet above sea level.

He laments that the mining development has not progressed faster:

Throughout this whole mineral region, strewn with promising mines as it is, not more than ten properties are being now developed and not a single mill is doing anything to add to the bullion product of the world. If this belt were in California, the cheerful clatter of the stamps would awaken the echoes on every hillside and canyon, and all would be bustle and clatter where now is solitude. Yet I venture to assert that in no place in California can ores be treated more cheaply than in this favored region. For all indication, there is little doubt the patient miners and prospectors will not have to wait much longer for their year of jubilee.[22]

This traveler also noted that there were a few women in the mining districts and that some had prepared an excellent camp.

At the time of this visit, there were as many as 200 miners and ranchers in the area--enough to warrant the establishment of the first U. S. Post Office in the Catalinas. This post office was located at the American Flag Ranch, which had been built by Issac Lorraine in 1881. After a few years, dissension arose between the American Flag and the Acadia Ranch (located in what is now Oracle) about the name of the post office. Since the U. S. Post Office did not like towns with two names, they finally decided to call the area Oracle, and the post office was moved to Acadia Ranch. The Acadia Ranch currently serves as the headquarters of the Oracle Historical Society.

The miners' need for lumber encouraged a fledgling timber business. Louis Ziegles operated the first steam powered saw mill in Alder Canyon in 1891. His crew sawed about 6000 feet of lumber every day for use in the mines and for homes in the San Pedro Valley. Eight to ten men were employed at his mill, plus that many more as loggers in the woods. They felled trees that were 150 to 200 feet in length and 2 to 8 feet in diameter. This sawmill was abandoned after a few years of operation.[23]

One of the few attempts to develop mines on the south side of the Catalinas was made by Col. C. P. Sykes at the Sabino Canyon mines in 1892. According to the local papers, he believed that he had struck a "bonanza" and that Tucson was on the verge of experiencing the "biggest mining boom known to the history of Arizona."[24] The anticipated riches from these mines did not develop although the Pontatoc mine in the southwestern part of the range produced 5,000 ton of low grade copper between 1907 and 1917.[25]

The mines of the Catalinas and the legend of the "mine with the iron door" attracted Col. William F. "Buffalo Bill" Cody. In 1909, he bought and leased several mines including Campo Bonito and Southern Belle. He hired men to help mine gold, silver and tungsten, but his mines were only marginally successful, and he later suspected he may have been hoodwinked by purchasing mines that had already been "worked out." One of Cody's claims did yield a jaguar hide. When the workers at his mine discovered their burros were being killed, they set a trap and caught a large male jaguar. His hide was delivered to Cody and became one of his prized possessions.[26] Cody's mining company closed after his death in 1917.

One of the owners of the Southern Belle and other mines in the area was a mid-westerner--General Elliott Warren Rice. Mount Rice, overlooking both of the old mining districts, is named after this prospector.[27]

16

Mining on the north side of the Catalinas continued well into the twentieth century. Minerals that were discovered in the Catalinas included silver, gold, lead, zinc, scheelite (a source of tungsten) and copper. Certainly valuable ores were mined and money was made, but the production of the mines in the Catalinas did not compare to the high hopes of area residents in the 1880's and 1890's. The mines did hasten the timber industry and the development of roads helped open the area for additional recreational use.

Chapter Three

EARLY HOMESTEADS AND RANCHES

Permanent settlement in these mountains began at about the same time as the first mines were developed. The first successful homestead was made by Emerson Oliver Stratton in 1880. He and his wife and children resided permanently on a ranch near Marble Peak. One of their sons, John Simeon, who had the distinction of being the first anglo child born in the Catalinas, was delivered by Stratton himself since the midwife did not arrive in time for the event. The family lived in a dugout until their first house was built, consisting of one room and a lean-to kitchen. Much of the Strattons' food came from the Catalinas. Stratton hunted throughout the area and was a crack shot, often felling a deer with a single bullet through the heart. He provided his family with other meat, including rabbit, squirrel, quail, dove and occasionally bear. They butchered cattle from their ranch, found honey in hollow oaks and made jams and jellies from the wild grapes and mulberries that grew in creek bottoms.

Stratton admitted that his early ranching there "did not amount to much" and he fittingly called his ranch Pandora. He was interested in mining and staked a claim on a copper mine he called the Commanche. He supported his family by working for the Santa Catalina Company, where he assessed claims, helped build roads, and supplied beef to the mining camps.

Stratton deeply appreciated the natural environment of the Catalinas. He recalled that tall grass grew all over the northern slopes of the Catalinas and that poppies and mariposa lilies carpeted the ground. Stratton explored several of the caves in the area, finding one with a great chamber as large as two houses. Shortly after he first saw the caves, vandals shot and destroyed some of the many beautiful stalactites and stalagmites. He roamed the entire range of the Catalinas and once transplanted mint plants to a damp spot near Sabino Canyon where they rooted and lived for many years. Rattlers were numerous and Stratton reported that it was not unusual for him to kill ten to twelve rattlers on a trip from his ranch to Oracle and for dogs and horses to be snakebitten. The Strattons stayed on their ranch until 1895.[28] Today's maps show a spring, a saddle and a canyon named after Stratton.

Robert N. Leatherwood had a ranch and an orchard near the Strattons. Leatherwood became the first mayor of Tucson in 1880 and later served as sheriff from 1894-1898 and as a territorial legislator for three terms. He called himself an "unreconstructed rebel" and was responsible for establishing the first Tucson speed limit (5 mph) for horses. He got his start in the orchard business in the Catalinas when he picked up a wagon load of fruit trees from a man from California who could not sell them to anyone else in Tucson. Leatherwood eventually learned the tricks of grafting to develop superior fruit and had the finest peaches, pears, apricots, apples and quince for miles around.[29] He sold both fruit and vegetables to the neighboring mining camps. Like Stratton, Leatherwood developed several mines in the area. He and Stratton were partners in the Apache Camp mine until they quarreled, ending their business relationship. Leatherwood eventually sold his mines to the Copper Queen Consolidated Mining Company, but he asked to live near his orchards and to remain as caretaker of the mines. His wish was granted and he lived for many years in a pineboard cabin on Rattlesnake Gulch. The cabin had been built with the first boards brought down from the sawmill on the north side of the Catalinas. During the last few years of his life the cabin fell into ruins and he lived in a tent in his beloved orchards. Leatherwood continued to ride his horse to Tucson long after the time when there were quicker means of getting there, often spending three days just to get to town. He remained at Apache Camp until his death in 1920. In his obituary, he was remembered for his generous hospitality to anyone who happened to need shelter in his part of the Catalinas.[30]

The lush grasses and open space of the Catalina foothills were ideal open range for livestock and several ranches were established in these areas. One of the most famous was Steampump Ranch owned by George Pusch, near the ridge that still bears his name. A steam operated pump brought up water from a well for his livestock as well as that of many other ranchers who drove their cattle through this area. Persons traveling between Oracle and Tucson often made a stopover for one night at Steampump Ranch where they might change horses before proceeding on to their destination. Other well known ranches on the west side of the Catalinas were those owned by Francisco Romero and William Sutherland. Each rancher is remembered today by place names in the area - Romero Canyon and Sutherland Wash.

Two of the older ranches in the southern foothills later became well known guest ranches--the Flying V, located west of Sabino Canyon, and the Rillito Ranch which is today called the Tanque

Verde Guest Ranch. Ranches in the northern foothills near what is now Oracle included the COD, the American Flag, the Kannally, the Cherry Valley, Linda Vista and the 3C. Nearly all the ranches in the Catalina foothills were cattle ranches although there were some areas that supported sheep.[31]

Chapter Four

THE NAMING OF MT. LEMMON

In 1881, the highest peak in the Catalinas got its name as a
result of a honeymoon spent in these mountains. In 1880, Sara
Plummer married Dr. John Gill Lemmon, who was a botanist at
the Lemmon Herbarium of Oakland, California. They had met
in Santa Barbara, where Miss Plummer had been the proprietress
of a small library which she considered to be "a haven for
intellectual development." John Lemmon was a frail man,
having never fully recovered from being a Civil War prisoner at
Andersonville. During his long recuperation, he had discovered
several new species of plants in California and hoped to find
new species in Arizona. They had planned a "botanical
wedding trip" to study the flora of Arizona.

The Lemmons were determined to climb the Catalinas from the
south side. General Eugene Carr, the founder of Ft. Lowell, and
Cyrus G. Pringle, a fellow botanist, warned them that no anglo
had ever passed over the southern rim of the mountains and
that, until very recently, the area had been a stronghold of the
Apaches. This did not deter them, and they spent a few weeks
in the spring of 1881 living on the south side of the mountains

in a stick and mud cabin. The cabin had been recently abandoned by a horse thief and was at least a mile from the nearest water supply. They later discovered a small cave which they set up as home, suspending their rations on a cord stretched across the ceiling to protect their food from packrats. Each day, Sara dressed in a short heavy suit with firm calfskin shoes and leather leggings to protect herself from the cacti and snakes as they tried new ways up the mountains. After several unsuccessful tries, they finally gave up and decided to try the north side.

Tucson Mayor Robert Leatherwood had suggested to the Lemmons that they should ask E. O. Stratton for assistance. When they arrived at Oracle, they were met by Alexander McKay who loaned them a burro to get to the Stratton Ranch. Stratton's wife was delighted with their visit since she had not seen another woman for eight months. Stratton recalled that the first time he saw the Lemmons, John was riding the burro and Sara was walking behind.

Stratton took them up into the mountains on his horses. Near the top, they travelled without trails, walking ahead and leading their horses as they crashed through the brush. At the top of the highest peak, Stratton carved all three of their initials on a pine tree, and all signed their names to a register which they placed in a tin can for protection. This register stayed on the mountain for almost 20 years until it was stolen. The tree with their initials blew down after the turn of the century. Stratton named the highest mountain in the Catalinas Mt. Lemmon in honor of Sara Lemmon since she was the first anglo woman to climb to the peak. Ms. Lemmon was 45 years old when she accomplished this feat.

All three of them were surprised to discover mule tracks near the top and followed them to two crude cabins near present day Summerhaven. There they found two old, half-starved hunters who had spent the winter and were shocked to see a woman at that elevation. The men were Ira Carter and William Reed, the first residents of the area that was later to be known as Summerhaven. Carter and Reed were homesteading 160 acres under the Timber Homestead Act, but bad weather, too little demand for timber and no roads to get the timber to market forced them to abandon their homestead shortly after the Lemmons' visit. Carter continued to visit the Catalinas, however, and the local paper reported that in 1885 he saw two bears, a fine mountain lion and two deer during a ride in the Catalina foothills.[32] Carter's name is remembered today in Carter Canyon, a small canyon located in the Summerhaven area.

While the Lemmons collected plants, Stratton hunted. He killed ten deer with eleven shots and several wild turkeys. He planned to give all of the meat to Carter and Reed, but a mountain lion dragged away one of the deer in the night. The Lemmons discovered six new plants during their excursion in the Catalinas, including a milkweed, a mustard, a spurge, a fern and two sunflowers.[33] John Lemmon was delighted to see the Arizona pine, a variety of the Ponderosa pine for which he had been searching. After their trek into the Catalinas, the Lemmons traveled to the Huachuca and the Chiracahua Mountains where they discovered more plants. All of their botanical discoveries were accredited to J. G. Lemmon, probably giving Sara Lemmon less credit than she deserved. In 1905, on their 25th wedding anniversary, they returned to Tucson, found Stratton, and once again the trio climbed Mt. Lemmon.[34]

The second recorded assault on Mt. Lemmon by anglo females occurred in August of 1887, when Mrs. Edwin Dodge and Mrs. George Kitt accompanied by E. O Stratton, climbed the mountain. The sight, they agreed, was "exceedingly grand."[35]

A few years after the Lemmons' visit, in May 1887, a strong earthquake hit the Catalinas, surprising the few residents who were there. The quake struck during the dry season and rocks tumbling on dry grass caused friction fires throughout the Catalinas. The local paper reported on this unusual event:

> When the quake struck...great slices of the mountain gave away, and went tumbling down the canyons, huge clouds of smoke or dust ascended into the sky...At three separate points, separate from three to five miles, clouds of dust were seen to rise above the mountain crest which would indicate that great ruptures had taken place. Over the summit of Mount Lemmon, the highest peak of the Catalinas, for quite awhile after the shock hovered a high dark canopy of smoke or dust until it gradually faded away...Great boulders...wrested from their seats from the shock, came thundering down into the valley, bounding over rocks and cutting their way through the air.[36]

Another report of this quake came from a Yaqui Indian who was in the mountains when it occurred. On a previous trip, this Indian had found a "rich placer in a gulch in the Santa Catalina mountains, where nuggets of gold as large as peas could be picked up." On the day of the quake, he had returned to the site with burros and supplies, prepared to work his claim. Just as he started to work, the "devils" made the "earth dance and great peaks of the mountains came tumbling down, killed his burro and frightened him nearly to death." After the quake, the Yaqui refused to go back and would not tell anyone where the site was.[37]

A glimpse of the Catalinas from the perspective of Tucsonans about a decade after the Lemmons' visit is shown in Map 3. Many current place names appear on this map although there are some interesting exceptions. Carter's Camp is shown in the are that is now Summerhaven. Mt. Lee was later named Kellog

Mountain. Mt. Scott may have been an earlier name for Green Mountain. The only route to Tucson was the road that ended at the sawmill, winding through the mining districts and down the northern slopes. No other trails or roads into the mountains existed.

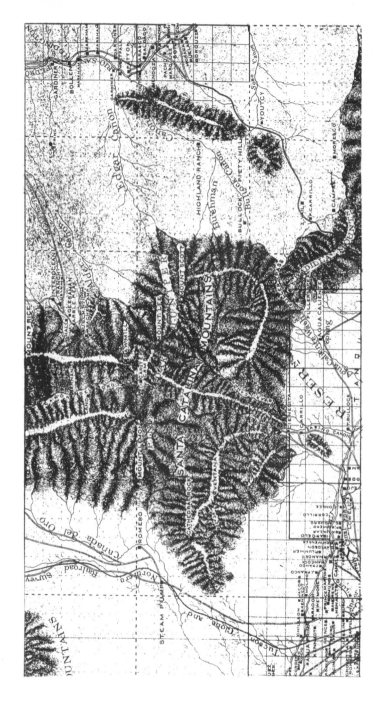

MAP 3 - 1893 MAP OF THE CATALINAS BY GEORGE J. ROSKRUGE

Chapter Five

TRAIL CONSTRUCTION AND THE U.S. FOREST SERVICE

The few people who lived in the higher elevations of the Catalinas at the turn of the century wanted easier access to Tucson to help them get timber and minerals to market or to help them obtain supplies for their own use. And even as early as 1881, some people began to recognize the potential of the area for recreation. In that year, the possibility was described in the local paper:

> when adequate accommodations can be secured, there is no doubt the region will largely be resorted to by the ladies of Tucson who seek to escape the tropical climate of our heated time. Wherever the ladies go, the gentlemen will follow and thus an attractive society will be gathered; and the expense of a long and tedious trip to distant states will be averted.[38]

One obvious solution to satisfy many needs was a trail up the south side of the mountains, which would facilitate travel between Tucson and the mountains.

In the late 1890's, Frank Weber (possibly with William Kellog) had established the second homestead on Mt. Lemmon and had built a cabin near the junction of Carter and Sabino Canyons in an area that was then called the Old Cabbage Patch. In October 1896, Weber came to Tucson to try to get local businessmen to donate money to help build a trail from Tucson to the top of the mountains. Faculty members from the University of Arizona soon promised him $75 of the $200 he would need for this venture. The advantages of the trail envisioned by Weber were explained in the local paper:

> (Weber) can construct a trail so as to bring the top of the mountain within eight miles of the Ft. Lowell road and about eighteen or twenty miles from Tucson...One could then leave Tucson, say on a Saturday afternoon, reach the top of the mountain by nightfall, enjoy a day amid the most magnificent hunting and fishing grounds in the territory and return to Tucson in time to resume business life on Monday morning. This arrangement would keep many persons at home who go abroad for a change of air.[39]

A follow-up story of Weber's visit appeared six weeks later. Weber apparently got at least enough money to buy provisions and left on a trip to scout out the new trail. He was expected to return to Tucson within two weeks, but after not returning in six weeks his long absence caused alarm because a heavy snowstorm had occurred in the mountains. A rescue party was sent out to look for him. Weber was found safe, and work on the trail soon began.[40]

The trail from Sabino Canyon to the summit was completed in 1897, and a second trail was started the same year. The purpose of these trails was to encourage "summer resorts for the Tucson folks."[41] This first trail went from Sabino Canyon to Sabino Basin, where some travellers spent the night, then on via the

Box Camp Trail to Soldier Camp. Early trails were built by clearing and blazing--notching the bark above the snowline to mark the trail.

Trail development and maintenance soon ceased being entirely a private venture and became the responsibility of the federal government. In 1902, President Theodore Roosevelt proclaimed the establishment of a forest reserve in the Santa Catalinas which covered more than 100,000 acres and created several jobs. In 1908, the President established the Coronado National Forest, which was comprised of the Santa Catalina, Santa Rita, Dragoon, Whetstone and Rincon Mountains. The forest was named, of course, for the Spanish explorer, Francisco Vasquez de Coronado, who journeyed through parts of the forest in the 1540's during his travels in the Southwest.[42]

Candidates for the first forest ranger positions were required to take a written exam and to pass a field test which entailed shooting a target with a rifle and a pistol. Twenty-three persons took this test in 1905. Col. R. C. McClure, Forest Supervisor from Silver City and administrator of the test, made notations such as "drunk" or "OK" on the list of candidates. Apparently, not all of the candidates were "OK." Those who survived the test and became rangers received $60 per month.[43] Within a few years the salary had nearly doubled, as described in this ad for rangers that ran in the Tucson Daily Citizen of September 1916.

Rangers wanted for U. S. Forest--to qualify for positions with the Forest Service, applicants must be between the ages of 21 and 40, be capable of enduring hardships and dangers, and passing a medical examination...The construction of cabins, telephone lines, and trails together with the performance of practical field work are included in the list of duties for which applicants must be qualified.

The examination is competitive. Rangers are started at an annual salary of $1100.

The rangers were expected to provide and maintain their own saddle and pack stock at their own expense.[44]

By 1906, the first trails proved inadequate, and major renovation was needed. The improvements were spearheaded by Robert L. Roger, who had been recently hired as a forest ranger. He pushed to get the trail system established throughout the mountains. Rogers and his boss, Catalina Supervisor T. F. Meagher, solicited funds for the trail, and within "less than twelve hours" they had collected the $600 they needed.[45] The trail improvements were made in about six weeks. By early July of that year, Meagher announced that the trail was ready and extended a "distance of six miles from base to summit." The opening of the trail was an event "worthy of genuine celebration" as it meant "a superb summer resort for Tucson and our people."[46]

Services sprang up immediately to accommodate the new trail. Ainsworth's Stables provided a stagecoach ride to Sabino Canyon with saddlehorses from there to the camp grounds at the top. Pack trains to Mt. Lemmon were offered by Fred Dabbs, just a few days after the trail was opened.[47]

Another ranger who helped get a better trail system was James Westfall who was hired in 1906 by the Forest Service to work in the Catalinas. Westfall had served in the Spanish American War and was a great mountain lover. He built a ranger's station near Oracle with the help of a small crew and his wife, Lita (sometimes called Barbara). In 1909, the Westfalls moved near what would later be Summerhaven where they would build the first inn on Mt. Lemmon in the 1920's.

JIM AND LETA WESTFALL (ON HORSE) AT SOLDIER CAMP, 1913.
(Courtesy of the Arizona Historical Society, Tucson, Arizona, #41354)

Today a trip to Mt. Lemmon is hardly newsworthy but at the turn of the century few enough Tucsonans made the trek up the mountains that records of their trips frequently appeared in the local press. In September 1904, the local paper reported that the Chamberlain and Huntsman families had returned to town after camping on Mt. Lemmon. The reporter added that in a few days "the last of the select crowd who have been on the mountain will have settled down in Tucson again."[48] In July 1909 a male school teacher spent some time on Mt. Lemmon and reported that his trip down by horseback took six hours to Sabino Canyon and another two hours to Tucson. He concluded that the trail was "certainly calculated to wear out the average traveler," and that the trip was "somewhat dangerous if made in the saddle." He also reported that there were "scarcely a dozen persons at Mt. Lemmon" when he left.[49]

Even trips to Sabino Canyon were newsworthy events on the society page. In 1908, this brief article appeared in the <u>Arizona Daily Star</u>:

> Sunday by a sort of common consent all the outing seekers headed for Sabino Canyon. Autoing parties out there were numerous and every livery team in the city was sold for the day to pleasure seekers who went up there. The roads were never in better condition and the more than 300 people who went up had a day of days.[50]

A brief drive started in 1908 to construct an "electric suburban line" from Tucson to Fort Lowell and through the ranching country to the foot of Mt. Lemmon. This concept was seen as another way to encourage Tucsonans to visit the mountains. The idea was debated for some time before being abandoned due to the cost of the project.[51]

More and better trails meant more visitors which caused the Forest Service officials to worry about fire hazards. The fire danger was often great during the early part of the summer before the rainy season began, and carelessness by campers could have been disastrous. The U.S.F.S built the Soldier Camp Cabin (although probably not in the area currently called Soldier Camp) to house fire fighting tools as well as firecrews.[52]

The need for even better trails was recognized after a severe forest fire scorched Alder Canyon and Peck Basin in 1910. With too few good trails or roads, fighting forest fires was impossible. Hobos were hired to fight this fire which lasted three weeks. Metal plaques, which read "remember the great fire of 1910", were placed on the big trees that still stood. Shortly after the great fire, federal money was available to build an extensive trail system throughout the Catalinas. These trails reduced the fire danger and also provided additional access for recreationists.[53]

SUMMIT OF MT. LEMMON WITH OLD FIRE LOOKOUT TOWER IN
BACKGROUND AND LOOKOUT TREE IN FOREGROUND, 1913. (Courtesy
of the Arizona Historical Society, Tucson, Arizona, #42097)

Fire lookout towers were placed at strategic points throughout
the Catalinas. These towers were unelaborate contraptions made
of pine. They were open at the top, with simply a railing
around the top platform. The towers swayed freely in the wind.
Some of the men in the towers communicated by using U.S.
Army surplus heliographic devices. Since the towers were
likely targets for lightening, protection was provided by a heavy
copper wire running up each leg and ending on a pole above the
tower. Ranger Gilbert Sykes who was stationed in such a tower,
recalled that the wires would start to hum and crackle and even

glow when the lightening got close. When that happened, he said it was time to get down because the lightening was about to strike. The efficacy of the protection system was demonstrated when the lookout at Lemmon Rock, which had been built by Jim Westfall in 1913, was replaced in 1934. As Gilbert Sykes and Jim Knagge finished the new lookout, they ran out of ground wire to protect it against lightening and stripped the old lookout of its wire. That night:

> ...a heavy lightening storm passed over the top of Mt. Lemmon. The old tower was struck. Three legs were shattered and the fourth was splintered...The next day the one split leg was cut through (before someone tried to climb it and got hurt) where upon the old tower fell over. It had stood through twenty one years of previous electrical storms when protected, but the first storm that caught it without protection was too much for it.[54]

A fifty-foot pine pole tower was built on Mt. Bigelow in 1916. When Gilbert Sykes served as a fireguard there a few years later, he lived close by in a dugout with a roof made of slabs of fir bark. The tower eventually burned down and was replaced by a metal one.[55]

Fire lookout trees supplemented towers throughout the area. These trees were marked with signs and some had large nails driven in their side for easy climbing.

In 1911, E. O. Stratton surveyed a new trail up the south side of the mountain which was called the Pine Ridge (or Palisades) Trail. It was a shorter and more direct trail, reaching the forest at a lower elevation than the old trail. Funds for the improvement of this trail were provided by the Forest Service, the Tucson Chamber of Commerce, Pima County and the Great Western Power Company. The Chamber of Commerce realized that better trails into the Catalinas would be good for business in Tucson as "people here will not go to the coast on their vacations but will stay in Arizona" and that Tucson would benefit since they would "spend their money here."[56] The trail was completed in May 1912, and a telephone line was installed along it so there was now phone service at the top of the mountain.[57] The public could use the phone, but had to make arrangements in advance with the phone company to relay messages throughout Tucson. The lower part of this trail is shown on maps today as Phoneline Trail. During many winters, storms broke the phone lines, and weeks of repair were required each spring. In 1912, the Chamber of Commerce offered the first trail map of the Catalinas, which is shown as Map 4.

A few years after the Palisades trail was opened, "seasoned mountaineer" E. L. Vail kept a detailed log as he ascended the trail:

We left Tucson at 6:30 in the morning making the run to the Ft. Lowell ranger station is just 30 minutes. At the Lowell station...we found good saddle horses and mountain mules for the trail...In ascending the trail from Sabino, one is impressed with the changes in the character of vegetation...For the first six miles of this trail...,one may have a view almost straight up and as nearly straight down...By the time the basin is reached, eight miles from the station, groves of billota, black oaks and an abundance of water appears. Horses may be watered at Ruby creek, a favorite camping place...The climb out of the basin is the steepest and hardest part of the journey as the trail twists back and forth on the mountainside between great boulders...Shortly one reaches the altitude of the manzanita bushes and finds them in the beauty of full bloom, with wild honey bees swarming about the blossoms...Finally, the trail strikes the ridge west of Pine Canyon ...we reach Mud Springs at noon stopping for luncheon. The water does not bear out the nomenclature

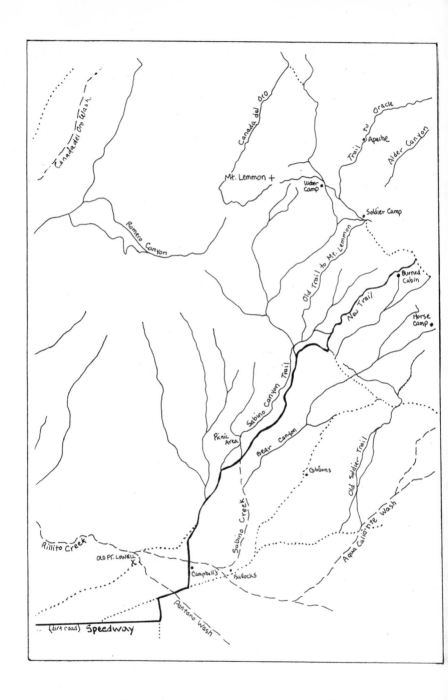

MAP 4 - 1912 **TRAIL MAP FOR THE CATALINAS**

of the spring, being clear, cold and delicious...The rather unattractive designation of the locality came from a huge spot of mud on the hillside below, which, in the driest season, always appears to be moist. A few sprigs of mint planted some years ago in this natural damp bed, by E. O. Stratton have spread into a fragrant patch of verdure of an acre or more in extent...Scattering pines begin to show up at Mud Springs...The distance from Mud Springs to Soldier Camp is seven miles, this part of the trail especially beautiful and cool, even in midsummer. It is shaded by pines, maple and douglas fir all of the way. When we were within a mile of Soldier Camp, snow commenced to fly. This was in early June...Snow fell all night, but the sight next morning when we looked out from the shelter...was easily worth the exertion of the trip.[58]

The townspeople soon realized that the Catalinas could also provide a superb site for a permanent summer camp facility. In 1914, 20 Boy Scouts went on a 15 day camping trip. Their primary goal during this trip was to build a log cabin which was to "be used as a nucleus for the YMCA summer camp for men and boys of Tucson." Perhaps the area they visited was near Oracle, as that is where the permanent YMCA camp was established in 1917.[59] The Catalina Council of Boy Scouts established Camp Lawton in 1921, in an area which would later be called Organization Ridge. By that time, there was a road of sorts to Soldier Camp. The scouts hiked three miles beyond the end of this road to their new camp. In 1923, the Business and Professional Women's Club announced it would soon purchase a summer home. Early plans for that camp included "shower baths, an electric light plant...and a motion picture open air theater."[60] The Girl Scout Camp--Whispering Pines--was not built until the 1950's. Recreation sites in other areas were also being planned. In 1918, the United States Forest Service created Bear Wallow Forest Camp, the first official recreation area in the Catalinas. They spent $100 to provide three picnic tables, one fireplace, one toilet, two register boxes, a hitch rail and a spring development.[61] At about the same time, some of the women who frequented the Catalinas proposed building a seven hole golf course at Soldier Camp; however, this development apparently never got beyond the planning stage.[62]

During World War I, Americans were urged to burn wood, reserving coal for the war effort. Although Tucsonans never burned much coal, the idea opened up the official use of the Catalinas as a firewood source. The Coronado National Forest allowed Tucsonans to cut green wood for seventy-five cents a cord, or dead wood for fifty cents.

Not everyone appreciated the work of the new forest service-- especially the ranchers who grazed cattle on what was now National Forest land. Much to the cattlemen's displeasure, the U. S. Forest Service required them to buy grazing permits and fined them if they trespassed onto government land without a permit. During the next several decades, the need to protect the Catalinas as a watershed area greatly reduced the amount of land made available for grazing.[63]

Feral livestock roamed the Catalinas well into the 20th century. As a youth in the 1930's, Glenn Mortimer of Oracle recalls rounding up cattle on the Catalinas northern foothills. There were many "slick eared" longhorns (meaning unbranded, without ear notches) freely roaming, which were easily obtained with the right technique. This method involved cutting off their horns and tying the animals to a bush where they would be left for a couple of days. The pain of the dehorning made them docile enough to lead down to a ranch when the cowboys returned.

Francis Knagge, whose family operated the pack train for the summer colonies, got a permit to graze cattle on the southern slopes of the Catalinas in 1939. He built more than twenty miles of trail up the steep slopes of Pontatoc, Finger Rock and Pima canyons so his cattle could get to more grass. Good portions of his trails are used by hikers today. His camp and corral were set up in what was then wilderness, but what is today about 100 yards from the end of Alvernon Way.

Chapter Six

ORACLE: THE CATALINAS' FIRST VILLAGE

Long before the first trails were built, Oracle was a thriving community located in the northern foothills of the Catalinas. At an elevation of more than 4500 ft., the terrain around Oracle was definitely mountainous with well defined seasons, including tolerable summers and an abundance of oak and manzanita.

By the 1870's, Oracle had become the center for several mining operations. It also quickly gained a national reputation as a health resort. In 1891, a physician wrote an article for a medical journal in which he concluded that the area could not be beaten for invalids and remarked about the abundance of fresh vegetables in the winter. He concluded that "game such as quail, antelope, deer, coyote, and wild hogs were plentiful. There was no dampness or sign of mould anywhere. The hours of sunshine were many."[64]

In the 1880's, one of the first winter resorts was founded in the Old Hat mining district near American Flag. Mr. and Mrs. Edwin S. Dodge, of Nova Scotia, and Jack Aldwinkle operated

MOUNTAIN VIEW HOTEL IN ORACLE--SOMETIME PAST ITS PRIME
BUT BEFORE IT BECAME A BAPTIST CHURCH. (Courtesy of the Arizona
Historical Society, Tucson, Arizona, #44086)

an adobe lodging house which they called Acadia Ranch. They
catered to many wealthy easterners, particularly health seekers
who believed that the area was one of the few places that
provided the "natural violet rays of the sun." From 1885-1901,
one room of the Acadia Ranch served as a U. S. Post Office.

In the early 1890's, the William Neal family started the
Mountain View Hotel in the area that had been the headquarters
for the San Pedro Cattle Company.[65] William Neal, who was
part black and part Cherokee Indian and had been one of
William "Buffalo Bill" Cody's scouts during the Indian wars,
owned the stage station at Oracle and carried mail to Oracle,
American Flag, Southern Belle and Mammoth. One of his most
dangerous jobs was carrying gold bullion from the Mammoth
mines to Tucson. He used different routes and sometimes
brought along his wife Annie to camouflage the real purpose of
his trips to Tucson. Annie, who was also of mixed ancestry,
"possessed unusual charm, culture and refinement and she ran

the hotel with an elan that put the hostelry among the leading Arizona lodges of that day."[66] Annie was a Catholic and had been given permission by the church to baptize babies. She also provided a private school for the children of the hotel guests.[67]

The Mountain View Hotel was made of adobe with twelve large bedrooms and a recreation room for dances. The opening of the hotel, on Washington's Birthday in 1895, was a gala event that drew wagons, buggies and buckboards filled with guests from all over Southern Arizona.[68] Many of the guests who followed were healthseekers who had tuberculosis or asthma and had chosen the foothills of the Catalinas as a place where they hoped to get well. The Mountain View Hotel still stands, although minus its porches, and now serves as a Baptist Church.

There was great rivalry between the Acadia Ranch and the Mountain View Hotel. One of the curious customs that developed was the half hour's difference in time between the two hotels. In Mammoth, just twelve miles away, time was half an hour earlier than at the Acadia's and one hour earlier than at the Mountain View.[69] In addition to the two hotels, at the turn of the century the village of Oracle boasted a general store, a stone church and two or three private homes and was surrounded by several ranches some of which stretched up into the Catalinas.[70]

In the early 1900's "Buffalo Bill" Cody was a frequent visitor to the Mountain View Hotel. He entertained visitors by shooting blocks of wood or glass balls thrown into the air from the hotel's porches. In 1912, he played a role for which his long white hair suited him well--that of Santa Claus for the children of the Catalina Mountains. The day was perfect, with a sprinkling of snow on Apache Peak to achieve the Christmas spirit.

BUFFALO BILL PLAYING SANTA CLAUS FOR THE CHILDREN OF THE CATALINAS, CIRCA 1912. (Courtesy of the Buffalo Bill Historical Center, Cody, Wyoming)

Children and parents came from all directions through the mountain passes and trails, some on horses, some on burros, in wagons and all sorts of conveyances...Promptly at noon, the arrival of Santa Claus in Campo Bonito was announced and he appeared by the Christmas tree. The words of Santa Claus although spoken in kindly tones were strange to all present and not until afterward was it learned that the greetings of Santa Claus were in the tongue of the Sioux Indians and told of the Sioux conception of the Great Spirit that sent Santa Claus to gladden the hearts of the children of the world. After the many gifts had been dispensed, sports were in order and the balance of the afternoon was taken up in foot races for the little boys and girls, in burro races, shooting matches, etc...Col. Cody has won fame in many lines but the little children of the Catalina mountains will always remember him as a dear old Santa who gave them lots of toys.. and love and good cheer among the rugged canyons and defiles of the Catalinas.[71]

George Stone Wilson came to Oracle in 1906 as a young man in hope of regaining his health in the Arizona sunshine. When he arrived, all eighteen guests of the Mountain View Hotel came out to greet him as he got off the stage. He later married and bought a ranch on the northern slopes of the Catalinas which he called Rancho Linda Vista. The Wilsons' life was probably not much different than that of the other ranchers in the Catalinas at the time. They went to Tucson in a wagon to shop, often driving at night in the summer to avoid the heat. Their entertainment included bridge and poker, a phonograph, guitars, occasional boxing matches at Mammoth and a monthly dance at the Mountain View Hotel. Ms. Wilson was a good shot and provided the family with doves, deer, quail and other game. Often being gone weeks at a time, Wilson rounded up his cattle and drove them to Tucson, camping the first night at Oracle Junction and the second night at Steampump Ranch.[72]

A severe drought in 1922-23 caused great hardships to all ranchers in the area and the Wilson's were no exception. In 1924, at the suggestion of their friend, Harold Bell Wright, they turned Rancho Linda Vista into a "dude" ranch. Cottages were added to accommodate guests who wished to enjoy horseback riding, tennis on a dirt court and trap shooting, as well as the spectacular scenery. There was even a phone. Some of the guests "roughed it" by helping with work around the ranch [73] In the 1920's, an airstrip was added to accommodate that era's "jet set" visitors. Among the guest list was Countess Dorothy Di Frasco, who "created the greatest stir when she arrived with her silk sheets, fantastic wardrobe and jewels, black riding habit and side saddle which she rode over the hills of Linda Vista."[74]

Many Rancho Linda Vista visitors relished the horseback ride to Coronado Camp, which was the setting for Harold Bell Wright's 1922 novel, The Mine with the Iron Door. Wright had come to Tucson in 1915 in the hope of recovering from tuberculosis. He rigged up an elaborate camp in the southern slopes of the Catalinas, where he lived in the sunshine. He met some German miners who had some gold and were very secretive about where it came from.[75] This meeting and the persistent myth about the hidden gold in the Catalinas inspired his novel. The spot Wright chose to do his writing was an isolated part of Rancho Linda Vista. All of Wright's supplies had to be taken in by pack horses. George Wilson visited him weekly during that three-month period while Wright wrote the book and recalled "If I didn't find him writing out under a tree he would be out panning gold or looking for wild hogs in the brush."[76]

In 1925, the movie "Mine with the Iron Door" was made in the Oracle area. While setting up one of the scenes, a laborer found a gold nugget the size of a pea. When the others on the set saw it, all work stopped for two days while everyone, including the cast, hunted in vain for more gold.

HAROLD BELL WRIGHT WRITING AT HIS DESK AT HIS CAMP IN THE CATALINA MOUNTAINS. (Courtesy of the Arizona Historical Society, Tucson, Arizona, B#32,354A)

George Wilson remembers cordial relationships with the forest rangers who were probably more lenient than rangers today. He recalled going deer hunting in the Catalinas with a friend. After three unsuccessful days, their hunger drove them to stun fish in a stream with a gunshot--an illegal fishing technique. After catching about 15 fish in this manner, he noticed a forest ranger observing him. The ranger did not fine him, but stayed the night enjoying an enormous feast of fried fish.[77]

Rancho Linda Vista survived the Depression years and continued as a guest ranch until 1950. The area now serves as a quasi-commune for a number of professionals, including artists and teachers.

Elizabeth Lambert Wood lived in the Oracle area since 1902, coming to Arizona for the health of her tubercular husband. Ms. Wood was a frequent guest at the Mountain View Hotel where she met Buffalo Bill Cody's wife. She managed to learn from Mrs. Cody that Buffalo Bill's long white hair was actually a wig.[78]   She gave her land in Peppersauce Canyon to the Salvation Army and in 1948, donated her ranch, the Crooked G, to the Y.M.C.A. who renamed it the Triangle Y. The ranch was located in the Old Hat mining district. Wood later wrote several books based on her reminiscences about the area.

Chapter Seven

THE FOUNDING OF SUMMERHAVEN

At the turn of the century, Tucsonans had few means of escaping the summer heat except to stay inside during the day and to sleep outside at night. Although the evaporative cooler had been invented in 1908, it was not widely available until the early 1940's. Tucsonans who hoped for growth, but feared that the terrible summers kept newcomers away, saw a solution in the Catalinas. As explained in the Citizen,

> We must remember that there are four months of the year during which the heat to our first year visitor at least, is something to be looked forward to with considerable misgivings, if not with actual trepidation. It behooves us therefore to look about for some means of keeping the visitor with us throughout his first summer...The natural process of logic having led us unerringly to this conclusion, all that we have to do is raise our eyes to the glorious Catalina range, and our problem is solved.[79]

Several sharp businessmen realized that, sooner or later, a road would be built to the top of the Catalinas. They knew that the sweltering desert summer would assure a strong demand for summer homes in the cool pines as soon as that road was ready. Consequently, they began to prepare for the inevitable boom of cabin building and resort development.

In 1915, the Summerhaven Land and Improvement Company was formed by John F. Hankins, F.E.A. Kimball, Ira E. Huffman, B.F. Morris, Charles A. Thomas, John B. Ryland, R. B. O'Neil, J. B. Toohey and J. Edward Owen, with E. W. Childs as president. Kimball would later have a great impact on the preservation of natural areas in the Catalinas. In 1916, the Company purchased the old Weber homestead which was patented in 1910, and appropriately named the area Summerhaven. Three cabins were built immediately--one of them belonging to Childs. By 1917, twenty additional cabins were being planned for this area, along with a hotel and a lake.

The ever-enterprising James Westfall started the first sawmill in Summerhaven, known as the Mt. Lemmon Lumber Company. It supplied the builders with lumber so that cabins did not have to be made of primitive looking logs.[80] Since there was no road to Summerhaven, it took more than two months to move a huge three ton boiler (possibly the one abandoned by Louis Ziegles at Alder Canyon) over tracks that had been laid to its site at the mill. Edwin Knagge, who helped move the mill reported that "we laid tracks on the slopes of the hills and winched up the heaviest equipment" with the rest packed up by burros.[81] The Forest Service allowed the sawmill to operate as long as the only trees cut down were those making room for natural growth and that the lumber was used only for building in these mountains.[82] Every fall the closing of the mill's eight-month season was marked by the blowing of a deafening whistle, startling the wildlife and whoever else was there to hear it.[83] Westfall built a cable system to transport lumber from the mill to the mines, but the first load of lumber burned up the cable, and it was not used again.[84]

Supplies for Summerhaven were brought up on the southern trails by a pack train operated by the Knagge family who served as a mobile "corner store" for the summer residents. John Knagge and three of his sons ran the operation from 1913 until 1918, carrying building materials, furniture, food, supplies and sometimes people on their burros, mules and horses. The Knagges owned over 40 mules and burros, running half of them at a time while the others grazed and rested. The Knagges served the 25 families who had cabins in the Catalinas and as well as the summer campers. Their headquarters was set up in lower Sabino Canyon, at the foot of the trail near the present day Lowell Ranger Station.[85] Edwin Knagge was one of the sons who worked in the business and was 16 years old when it started. He recalls the details of this family operation:

There were very few people on Mt. Lemmon in those days. They'd take their children out of school the first of June and they would keep them up there until the 15th of September when they went back to school...We packed food and stuff up there all summer..about two trips a week. We had a mule team and a wagon (as well as) horses and burros. The trail is still there..it's called the Plate Rail...I packed building materials up...sheetiron...lumber...wooden floorings...and tin roofs. I guess there were about 25 cabins on Mt. Lemmon at that time...It was hard work, lifting things, putting the diamond hitch on...and you had to be strong to do it. Each (one of us) would drive five to seven burros ahead. The burros would want to eat as they go along. You let them eat so much and then you make them move. I used to carry rocks along. (If) the burro would stick his head out, I'd throw a rock at him. We would make about 8 miles the first day...to get up there where it was cool.(for) the eggs, butter and bacon...But for freight and stuff, we just took our time...We packed building materials up there as long as the snow didn't stop us...My father and I had to go up

THE KNAGGE FAMILY AT THEIR CATALINA HEADQUARTERS, 1918.
(Courtesy of the Arizona Historical Society, Tucson, Arizona, #48850)

THE KNAGGE'S BURROS LOADED WITH SUPPLIES FOR
CABINOWNERS AND CAMPERS AT THE TOP, 1918. (Courtesy of the
Arizona Historical Society, Tucson, Arizona, #48849)

and rescue a couple of men...that went up to jump some mining claims...When they went up there, the weather was nice...(but) it started snowing and they broke into this ranger station and put the horses on the front porch...They couldn't get out. The snow had got that deep. It took two days to get to them and we had to break snow all the way...We used to cut (Christmas) trees and sell them in Tucson. We'd get a permit for 100 or 200 trees and then we'd just tie them together and put them on three or four animals and bring them down to Sabino Canyon and then get them to Tucson.[86]

In spite of the beauty of their spectacular surroundings, boredom sometimes got the best of the Knagge boys. On occasion, it is told, they literally ran down the trails to Tucson on a Saturday afternoon in search of some urban excitement.

As the summer population increased, so did the need for communication with the outside world. At this time, there was still only one phone on Mt. Lemmon, and a "phone girl" was chosen to answer the phone and relay messages. Mary Childs Cotten, daughter of Eugene Childs, was selected for this job because she "could leap over the rocks and get the people to the phone quickly." She was probably in her early teens at this time. Ms. Cotten describes this job:

The Forest Service put one of their phones outside our cabin on a big pine with a little roof over the phone. People in Summerhaven had two hours that the phone could be used to make outgoing calls. During the other times the phone could only be used for incoming calls or by the Forest Service. It was my job to answer the phone and get the person called there as quickly as possible. I took my responsibility gravely and practically flew to get the people to the phone.[87]

During this same period, mail was delivered to Summerhaven once a week by F.E.A. Kimball.

In addition to the mails and the phone, one other means of communicating with the rest of the world was used by Gilbert Sykes who was a ranger in the fire lookout on Mt. Bigelow from 1919 to 1920. Since Sykes and his father knew Morse Code, the younger Sykes used a hand mirror to send heliographic messages to his father at Tumamoc Hill southwest of downtown Tucson requesting that specific supplies be sent. Sykes recalled that "Dad had the code pasted on the wall and he could read me if I went slow enough. I would tell him what I needed and the next day the Knagge boys would haul it up to me."[88] The younger Sykes had been a wireless operator in World War I and had been taught by Marconi himself. He left the Forest Service for a few years to become a barnstormer, parachutist and aerial acrobat, but eventually returned to the Forest Service.

Chapter Eight

THE "BACK" ROAD

Summer visitors to the Catalinas had two choices of how to get to their campsite. They could take an 8-10 hour horseback ride via the trails on the south side face of the mountains, or they could drive to Oracle and up through the mining districts to where the road ended and there mount horses to take them up several miles of trails to a choice spot at the top.

By 1915, many people began to think that both of the ways to get to Mt. Lemmon were too inconvenient and that a road was needed all the way to the top. The first step was taken by a group of businessmen from the Tucson "luncheon club" who agreed to appoint a committee to explore the possibility of a road up the south side of the mountains. Although it was realized that the south side was much more difficult than a northern route, such a road would reduce the distance to the top from Tucson by about 30 miles. The principal argument for the road was to keep Tucsonans from going to the coast in the summer, thereby keeping $500 to $1000 in Tucson for every trip saved. Members of the committee included Forest Service Supervisor R. J. Selkirk, Forest Ranger Westfall, County

Supervisor D. S. Cochran and J. D. Matthews, Division Engineer of the Southern Pacific. The committee members made an eight day trek in the mountains to determine a feasible route. They decided that a road up the south face via Sabino, Pine and Bear Wallow Canyons was feasible, and a bond election was set to raise $100,000 for the road survey.[89] To help convince the public of the need for this road, a motion picture was made along the proposed route and was shown in local theaters. It included several shots of trout swimming in mountain pools and many forest scenes. Perhaps the film helped. The bond election passed by a narrow margin and in December at least part of the road was surveyed. However, when the cost of construction for this road became apparent, enthusiasm for this route waned.

In 1916, the argument for improving the already existing road up the north side of the mountains gained momentum. Some thought was given to a new road up the west side of Oracle Ridge, but the favored route was through the mining districts. This route proved to be the most feasible, since parts of the road had already been built by the copper companies and they would support the venture in hopes of lowering their freight costs. A portion of this road was in Pinal County, which meant that another county would share in the cost of construction. The Daily-Consolidated Copper Company agreed to build the section in Pinal County from the state highway through the 3-C Ranch and on to the Pima County line. The Stratton Copper Company had already built two miles of the remaining ten miles to Soldier Camp. Thus, the road was built by a coalition of the copper companies, Pima and Pinal Counties and the Forest Service. The last section of the road, from Summerhaven to Soldier Camp, was completed in 1920. The new route, which had been built in three years, made the mountains accessible to Tucsonans by a five-hour drive, although when conditions were bad, the trip could take eight hours or longer. At any rate, the new road was good enough to put the Knagge pack train out of business.

SIGN AT THE TOP OF THE MT. LEMMON CONTROL ROAD ANNOUNCING WHEN CARS WERE ALLOWED TO GO DOWN THE MOUNTAIN. (Courtesy of the Arizona Historical Society, Tucson, Arizona, #61357)

One small problem with the new road was that the last seven miles--from Stratton Camp to Soldier Camp--were only wide enough for one lane of traffic. The solution was to keep the road open only a few hours at a time for cars going in either direction which is why the road became known as the Control Road. From Stratton Camp, cars could go up at 8:00am, 11:00am, 2:00pm and 5:00pm. Cars leaving Soldier Camp could go down at 9:30am, 12:30pm, 3:30pm or 6:30pm. If people were ready to leave at any other time, they just had to wait until the road was opened or risk a $50 fine. At the control points at the top and bottom, visitors chatted as they waited for their time to move onto the road. At popular times like Saturday mornings, a long string of cars would wait at the bottom for their appointed hour.[90] The grade of the old road was steep, at places 16% to 18%, and it washed out easily, especially during the summer rainstorms. Many cars had difficulty getting over the rough road and Stratton provided water for overheated radiators in a barrel alongside the road.

Some of the big touring cars could not make the turns in the roads, and their drivers would sometimes have to stop and backup more than once to negotiate a curve.

The road inspired unusual publicity stunts. In 1920, a Tucson automobile dealer drove from Tucson to Soldier Camp--in low gear all the way--in a little over seven hours. This feat apparently demonstrated the ruggedness of his cars.[91] A year later, a Willys-Knight car, stripped of its fan, managed to drive the road to Summerhaven in only three and a half hours without overheating![92]

If one did not have a car or did not want to risk one's car over the rough road, there was soon another alternative to getting to the cool pines in the summer. In 1923, Elmer Staggs organized the Mount Lemmon Stage and Freight Line. With his Reo Speedwagon, he delivered passengers and supplies during two round trips a week. Passengers could board the stage in downtown Tucson at Steinfeld's store. When his truck arrived at the top, a good portion of the entire Summerhaven population turned out to greet it. Some of the cabin owners were lucky enough to have Staggs deliver their goods to their doorsteps. Staggs abandoned the service during the Depression, as demand lessened.[93] He later helped build Sanctuary Cove--an all faiths chapel in the desert northwest of Tucson.[94]

Chapter Nine

MAN AND WILDLIFE

Many botanists in addition to the Lemmons have been interested in the Catalinas' ecology. In the early 1900's, the Carnegie Desert Laboratory was built on Tumamoc Hill. The scientists who worked there brought species of plants from other countries and planted them on Mt. Lemmon to see if they could survive. Test plots were situated near Carter Canyon and Soldier Camp. It is not known whether any of these exotics escaped and are still growing in the Catalinas.[95]

In 1910, an unidentified entomologist and a botanist made a field trip into the higher elevations via the north side, accompanied by Robert Rogers who was then serving as deputy supervisor in the Forest Service. As they neared Oracle they spotted Lita Westfall, wife of the ranger at Soldier Camp and owner of the first lodge on Mt. Lemmon, who had been hunting dinner without success. She led them to their house and later the Westfalls took the scientists up the trail to the top. They were enthralled with the pine forests and cold streams with speckled trout. They had "butter for supper as some passing stranger had left two and a half pounds on the doorstep along with syrup, lard and other delicacies."[96]

Even before the new road was finished, it was recognized that the coming of cars to Mt. Lemmon would affect the wildlife in the area. In 1916, a Forest Service official discussed the potential problems with summer campers during a lantern slide talk on the subject of game protection.[97] That same year, the Forest Service decided that a wildlife census was needed to count the numbers of whitetail deer, elk, bear, mountain lion and big horn sheep, so they could monitor the effect of increasing human activity on these animals.[98]

The impact was already being felt. For example, acres of oak forests on the north side of the mountains had been destroyed at the turn of the century due to illegal cutting. The smelter in Mammoth required green wood because it burned hotter and loggers filled this need by taking many cords of green oak wood from the Catalinas. The loggers were fined thousands of dollars by the Forest Service when they were caught.[99] By 1916, there may have been only one herd of bighorn sheep left. The Forest Service tried to keep the location of the herd secret to help prevent their extermination, although most poachers seemed to know the sheep's whereabouts.

Wild turkeys had been abundant in the area before 1900. In fact, another name for the Soldier Camp area in the 1880's was Turkey Roost. Robert Leatherwood reported that he had shot many 40 pound turkeys there. By the turn of the century, however, the turkeys were gone, possibly due to natural causes such as forest fires or droughts, or to the killing and marketing of the birds by the Apache and Pima Indians. Turkeys were reintroduced into the area in 1919 by the Tucson Game Protective Association but they did not regain their former numbers.[100] After the turkeys were reestablished, however, coyotes appeared at the higher elevations apparently seeking out turkey dinners.

In 1918, 11,000 trout fry were planted in Sabino Creek near Carter Canyon and at Bear Wallow. The fry were supplied by the federal government and were transported in metal cans to Stratton Camp via a Blue Bar Taxi Cab. They were then packed on burros to their final destination.

This was not the first fish planting in the Catalinas although the details of the first planting are not certain. Local enthusiast for the Catalinas, Ted Knipe, reports that the first trout were added by Ed Vail and George Stratton in 1906 when they horse-packed rainbow trout into upper Sabino Canyon.[101] However, according to Ed Knagge, the first plant was made by Jim Westfall, Daniel MacDougal of the Carnegie Desert Laboratory and rancher Ed Vail some time before 1910.[102] In 1920, 12,000 trout fry were used to restock the streams under the leadership of F. E. A. Kimball. This time the fish were carried all the way up in a truck and were distributed at Bear Wallow and in various pools in Sabino Canyon.[103]

Although there were many streams and a few pools in the Catalinas, there were no naturally occurring lakes. In the 1920's, the cabin owners in the Soldier Camp area decided to correct that situation by creating tiny Soldier Lake in the 1920's. The idea of constructing a small dam in Bear Wallow Canyon is attributed to summer resident and County Supervisor Dave Cochran. Some members of the homeowners association balked at his idea but eventually a rock and masonry dam twenty feet high and thirty-six feet across was built by the association. Some cabin owners thought that only children should be allowed to fish in the lake but others did not agree. It was finally decided that the lake would be open to the public and that it would be regulated and stocked by the Arizona Game and Fish

Department.[104] The children of Soldier Camp joined the fish for swims on warm summer afternoons.

Sensitivity to the natural environment of the Catalinas continued to build. In 1928, Tucson printer and bookstore owner and state legislator, Frederick. E. A. Kimball, succeeded in getting the forest service to designate a 4464-acre Natural Area in the Marshall Gulch area. Part of the dedication of this area was held at the Mariposa Lodge, where 40 persons watched five reels of film on conservation which had been provided by the Forest Service. G. A. Pearson, director of the Southwest Forest Experiment Laboratory in Flagstaff, was one of the speakers at the dedication. He predicted that the natural area would become a "veritable mecca for research workers in plant and animal ecology" and emphasized that "aside from protection from fire and other destructive agencies, human interference must be restricted to a minimum."[105] Kimball, who had been called the patron saint of the Catalinas, died in 1930 and Kimball's Peak was named in his honor the following year. The only other natural area in the Catalinas was created in 1935, when a 1000-acre plot was designated the Butterfly Natural Area.[106]

In 1936, the Forest Service counted 36 remaining bighorn sheep on Pusch Ridge and in the Window Rock area in Ventana Canyon. Officials noted that there were only five lambs among them, concluding that the eagles were killing far too many of the young to guarantee survival. The Forest Service called for an end to sheep hunting to avoid extinction. Ironically, in the same newspaper edition describing this Forest Service count, another article appeared about hunting in the Catalinas. Its author described the sheep and the antelope as a lure for hunters from the East, as well as the joys of the popular sport of mountain lion hunting which had become the rage since 1920.[107]

Mountain lions in the Catalinas have always caused controversy. Some people, especially ranchers, believed that these dangerous beasts should be controlled due to their propensity to kill livestock and other native animals. Others, however, felt that the lions were part of the natural environment and should be preserved. Probably fewer people held the latter view during the early settlement of the Catalinas, however, and mountain lion hunting was considered quite acceptable. Billy Chester was one of the well known big game hunters. In the late 1920's Chester lived in the northern slopes of the Catalinas and worked on a guest ranch where he took visitors on lion hunts. In November 1931, he created a sensation in downtown Tucson as he drove in with a 175-lb. mountain lion strapped to his car, which he had just killed in the Catalina foothills. Chester was surprised to find big lions in the vicinity and conjectured that the cat had come down from the northern slopes to bask in the sun.[108] The next year he killed four lions which he believed were responsible for the deaths of 32 colts, several calves, and deer.

The Aberts squirrel, the tuft-eared one frequently seen today, was not a native of the Catalinas but was introduced from Flagstaff in 1940 and 1941. These squirrels soon became well established in the Summerhaven and Soldier Camp area. Beaver were planted in Sabino Creek by the Arizona Game and Fish Department in 1943. These beaver got to the Catalinas in a roundabout way. They were native to the Colorado River area and had first been moved to the Salt River Valley canals in central Arizona. Unfortunately, their lodges in the canals caused flooding so they were then moved to the Catalinas.[109] Unlike the Aberts squirrel, they did not thrive. Natural causes and hunters wiped out the small population within a decade.

Chapter 10

EVERYDAY LIFE IN THE SUMMER COLONIES

In 1910, Pauline Kitt Hull made her first trip into the mountains with her family to establish a summer camp. Unlike today, the camps then were fairly elaborate shelters that were designed to be lived in for several months. Many supplies were brought up including tents, silver, china, crystal, clothes and food. Ms. Hull recalled that her parents took her up the old Box Canyon Trail through Sabino Canyon. Small children were carried up in leather holders somewhat like saddlebags with one child on either side of the horse. Ms. Hull stated that "once you made the eight to ten hour ride up the mountain, you stayed all summer. The only ones who did any commuting were the husbands and they only came up for long weekends."[110] The Hull family spent the summer of 1910 at Bear Wallow and the summer of 1911 at Soldier Camp.

Dinners were held outside under the trees and were shared by many of the families camping in the area. A few of the dinners were fancy enough to require good linens and candlesticks. During the day, the women entertained themselves with bridge

CAMPING NEAR WEBER'S CAMP (NEAR WHAT IS NOW SUMMERHAVEN), 1900. (Courtesy of the Arizona Historical Society, Tucson, Arizona, #3578)

games and tea parties, while the children played tennis, explored the mountain on foot and on horseback, and dallied on the swinging bridge at Soldier Camp. Some of them ventured a few miles away to the old Leatherwood orchard where they could eat their fill of peaches and apples. Families gathered raspberries, blackberries, strawberries and gooseberries that grew wild throughout the mountains. Flowers were abundant including shooting stars, violets and lily of the valley. The families hauled water for washing, bathing and drinking from the creek at Soldier Camp.

In the evening, the only light came from candle flame or lantern glow, plus the moon and starlight, of course. Entertainment centered around a big campfire where the children sang and put on skits. The Forest Service later forbade the large campfires as they were considered too dangerous.

While nearly all the families who first summered in the Catalinas lived in tents, one family did not. The Joel H. Huntsman family built one of the first summer homes in the area in 1906. Huntsman was the Overland automobile dealer in Tucson. The Huntsman cabin was built in the Marshall Gulch area and remained there until 1960 when it was moved to make way for the picnic area. Remnants of their orchard can still be seen in the vicinity. When their cabin was built, the area was quite isolated, and the adventures faced by the family were not unlike those of other families in frontier areas. One of the Huntsman's children, Nancy Breazeale, tells her mother's story about an incident with a mountain lion that occurred in 1908:

We had a corral at the old cabin. A neighbor boy kept his burro in the corral with our horses. The burro didn't come in when our horses came charging back in the middle of the night. Mother knew something had happened to that burro but no one wanted to go out at night looking. The men were gone to Tucson at the time for supplies. Two days later, Mother was out riding. She was carrying a 30-30 which she always carried, but was low on bullets. Her little dog Captain was with her. He climbed into a thicket, came yipping out and headed lickety split for home. Mother thought there was something in the thicket, so she fired, hoping to scare off whatever was there. Joe Willard...came running up the trail...Together he and Mom went over to the thicket and sure enough there was this big pile of leaves with a little hoof sticking out. Signs pointed to the fact that the lion would be back. Mother and Mr. Willard went over to get Jim Westfall's big bear traps. During the short time they were gone the lion came back and chewed on the burro some more. They didn't set up the traps until mid-afternoon the next day to give Mr. Westfall time to get his hound dogs home. The following morning when they went over this big lion was caught by two toes and was lunging back and forth. They left Howard, the boy whose burro had been killed, with a light gauge rifle to watch...By the time they got back with the 30-30 , Howard had shot the lion. He was afraid it would tear its toes off and lunge at him...From the tip of its tail to the head it measured a full nine feet.[111]

When the dirt road up the back side of Mt. Lemmon was finished, the summer colonies began to grow. Homeowners in the Soldier Camp area at this time included Meade Clyne, James Dunseath, Stanley Kitt, Dave Cochran, John Ryland, E. G. Sporleder and E. VanderVries among others. The ranger's station and barns were also at Soldier Camp.

In the Summerhaven area, a few cabins were available for rent from the Summerhaven Land and Improvement District. These cabins boasted cook stoves, worktables and screened cupboards and rented for $35 a month. The old Weber cabin was still standing, but only the rock foundation and a few logs remained of the Carter cabin. The Mariposa Lodge, which was the first inn on Mt. Lemmon and had been built by the Westfalls in 1921, was the center of the little community. Cabin owners in the Summerhaven area included William Sawtelle, Judge Samuel Kingan, Herb Morrison, A. W. Olcott and Eugene Childs. The Summerhaven Land and Improvement Company published a brochure enticing Tucsonans to visit and assuring them the area could be reached in 3.5 hours over "an excellent highway". They also reported that trout were "waiting to be caught" and described "two wonderful caves of unknown extent which...reveal undreamed beauties."

The Tucson families that could afford summer homes in the Catalinas were fairly well-to-do, and the social activities of these families were described in the society page of the local paper. Many of the articles detailed trips made to Tucson by those who were spending the summer in the mountains, short trips made to the mountains by people living in Tucson, and weekend trips made by many Tucson businessmen to be with their families who were spending the summer there. Special social occasions were described in great depth in the Arizona Daily Star. They provide a detailed portrait of the summer life in the mountains in 1920:

--Asilosierra, the home of Mr. and Mrs. A. M. Franklin was the scene of a merry party given in honor of Miss Edith Failor. In a circle of large trees a camp-fire glowed, and logs to serve as benches were rolled close to the flames for greater comfort. The house was cleared for dancing and the porch was dimly lighted by a single lantern, making it ideal for moonlight waltzes...Popcorn and cookies furnished light refreshments. Songs and stunts, always popular and amusing, interested everyone. As the fire burned lower the guests reluctantly started homeward, all agreeing that it had been one of the most successful of the many enjoyable camp-fire affairs this season.[112]

--A merry party of young people made an enjoyable trip to Mt. Bigelow on Thursday afternoon. They rode horseback up to the peak where they dismounted and had lunch. Then they climbed the lookout tower, which gives a sweeping view of both the San Pedro and Santa Cruz river valleys.[113]

--A safe and sane celebration of the glorious fourth was hugely enjoyed by more than a hundred people from all over the state at Summerhaven. The flag and bunting decorated picnic ground was the scene of the festivity at the old Weber cabin. A barbeque "done to a turn" was prepared by Mr. Jim Westfall and large tables decorated with mountain wild flowers were spread under the pine trees by the ladies. A rare treat in the form of a freezer of ice cream was heartily welcomed. Further amusement was furnished by songs and stories.[114]

--The large and attractive cabin, Lucky Strike, of Mr. and Mrs. Ryland of Soldier's Camp, was the scene of a small impromptu dance last Saturday night. Mrs. Ryland invited all the young people from both camps to attend. The spacious front porch furnished a delightful dance floor and the hospitable glow of the fireplace attracted the young people during intermissions. Refreshing punch and delicious little cookies were hugely enjoyed as refreshments. The brilliant moon-light sponsored many delightful moon-light waltzes and everyone agreed that the whole affair was most successful.[115]

--A merry party of young people made a horseback trip to Wilderness of Rocks. They started in the morning and spent the day. At noon they stopped beside one of the streams, built a campfire and cooked a delicious meal. The Wilderness is a fascinating and dangerous place to explore and the young people returned tired but delighted with their trip.[116]

--Mr. and Mrs. Cartmell and their daughter, Miss Bobby Cartmell, entertained on Saturday night with the first watermelon party ever given in Summerhaven...Dancing was enjoyed in the early part of the evening and later the feature of the affair appeared. Huge watermelons "iced" in the cold mountain stream were cut in generous slices and greatly enjoyed by the guests.[117]

--Mrs. A. M. Franklin entertained a few ladies at an informal luncheon on Wednesday. The cottage was prettily decorated with bouquets of yellow columbine and clever place cards marked each guest's place and carried out the color scheme. The delicious luncheon daintily served was greatly enjoyed by the guests.[118]

--A moonlight "pie party" was a novel affair which offered amusement for the campers of the various mountain resorts on Friday night. All participants hiked over to Inspiration Point carrying many pies and keen appetites. An immense camp fire blazed from the rocky point and soon the delicious smell of boiling coffee was wafted to the hungry circle. After watching the moon rise the hikers cut the pies and poured out the fragrant coffee.[119]

--The many friends, both old and new, of Mr. and Mrs. Ray Jenkins entertained them by gathering for a farewell dance in their honor. The affair was decidedly novel as the young folk all came dressed in grotesque "tackey" representations of various types and kinds of people. A great campfire back of the cabin served as footlights and the audience was seated around it...Among the cleverly acted characters were a long, lean ghost, a rag doll, a dainty bride with her accompanying flower girl, a quaint Japanese lady, a modern Bohemian artist, a man dressed as a black "mammy", a girl as an Alpine guide, a gay spring maid, a wood fairy, a merry cowgirl and a daring gypsy. The house and porch, dimly lighted, were used for dancing. A Victrola supplied music and delicious punch and cookies were served for refreshments. At the end of the successful affair, the guests gave a yell for their host and hostess and reluctantly bade them goodbye.[120]

One of the women who was occasionally mentioned in the society pages was Lita Westfall. Unlike most of the other women, she was a permanent resident of Mt. Lemmon. She was a strong and rugged woman who some say had a fairly heavy beard and had one blue and one brown eye. By the 1920's her escapades had turned her into a legend in the Catalinas. One oft-told tale concerns a dispute she had with Elmer Staggs, who operated the freight line. After he delivered her order of flour, she discovered that the sack had been saturated with kerosene during the trip up the mountain. She located Staggs, who happened to be standing under the balcony of her lodge, and promptly dumped the contents on his head. On another day, as she was delivering her husband's lunch on a burro, she encountered an aggressive bear. Fortunately, she had brought her gun and she killed the bear instantly. The bear skin was displayed for a time in a sporting goods store in Tucson then later was hung with the gun in her lodge, where it remained until the lodge burned down.

George Stone Wilson of Oracle knew Ms. Westfall and remembered her as a robust woman who could lay adobes, shoe horses and do carpenter work. He concluded:

> She was a fine gal but a little on the rough side. I remember one day when I rode over to the ranger station and saw her trying to ride a bronco mule. The mule would throw here every time she got on him. I rode up to her and said "Mrs. Westfall, let me try riding that mule for you. She looked at me and said "George Wilson, you get the hell out of here. I am going to ride this XXX if it breaks every bone in my body" and she eventually rode him.[121]

Since Jim Westfall was busy with his duties in the Forest Service, much of the work of running the Mariposa Lodge fell to Lita Westfall. The 40'-by-40' lodge provided meals and sleeping accommodations. The partitions between the rooms in the lodge did not reach the ceiling, but apparently the guests did not mind the lack of privacy.

There were rumors that Ms. Westfall made and served liquor to guests during Prohibition. Ruth Stewart, who was a friend of hers, once asked her why she didn't kill the skunks that lived under the lodge. Ms. Westfall explained that she liked to keep the skunks around for the fall when she made her mash. If she feared anyone might smell her brew, she would kill a skunk to cover up the odor. Ms. Stewart, herself, admitted drinking some fine homemade wine which Ms. Westfall had made from native elderberries.

The Westfall's Mariposa Lodge finally began to have some competition from the Neoli Lodge, which was constructed at the corner of Carter Canyon and Douglas Street. It was owned by three bachelors who vowed that the first one who got married would forfeit his interest to the other two. The lodge's name was made from the scrambled letters of the last name of one of the bachelors, R. B. O'Neil. Their pact was solemnly regarded, forcing one of the bachelor owners, Charles Stewart, to keep his engagement a secret until he could sell his interest in the lodge.[122]

Charles Stewart's wife, Ruth, first visited the mountains in 1924. F.E.A. Kimball asked her to look after some cabins at Summerhaven which she did in exchange for a place to stay. Eventually the Stewarts bought a cabin in Summerhaven that they dearly loved in spite of the fact that the "society" was in Soldier Camp. One of Ruth Stewart's fondest memories was visiting a favorite picnic spot in the Marshall Gulch area which was reached via a rough and beautiful trail. After a picnic, she would take soap and a towel and head for a place in the stream surrounded by rocks, which she called "Cleopatra's Bathtub."[123]

Those Tucsonans who enjoyed the mountains but did not wish to stay at the lodges began to clamor for more building sites in the Catalinas. Other than the 160 acres originally homesteaded and later bought by the Summerhaven Land and Improvement District, nearly all of the land was controlled by the Forest Service. The Term Lease Law, which had been passed in 1915, allowed the Forest Service to lease five-acre plots for ten to twenty-five dollars per year for a maximum of thirty years. By 1916, the Forest Service had received 50 inquiries about such leases in the Catalinas, even though they were not yet available.[124] After a careful study, they decided that the entire area could host 500 cabins. The first permits for summer homes on forest land were offered in 1918. In 1920, the Forest Service laid out 40 lots in the Soldier Camp area, 22 in Upper Sabino and 12 in Lower Sabino. By the early 1930's, 57 of the 95 lots laid out were in use.[125]

The leased areas were divided into four districts: Soldier Camp, Upper Sabino Canyon, Carter Canyon and Middle Sabino Canyon. In 1923, the lessees in each district were: Soldier Camp - Mrs. Ernestine R. Griffith, Gilbert and Glenton Sykes, Joe Conway, Robert Benzie, W. T. Robie, Robert Cairn, E. A. Staggs, Mrs. T. Ed Litt, John Ryland, R. B. Savage, John Mets, Stanley Kitt, M. H. Starkweather, S. D. Gromer, Mrs. Edith Locker, Arthur C. Jacobson, Mrs. K. Jaynes, D. S. Cochran, R. Rasmessen, E. A. Vail, James R. Dunseath, L. H. Hofmeister, Dr. Meade Clyne, E. G. Sporleder, R. W. Place, Dr. S. H. Watson, E. VanderVries, Ralph W. Evans, Gerald Jones, Paul Rebeil, William Lindenfield and Mrs. Charlotte Harding; Middle Sabino - David W. Bloom, J. Cress Myers, Mrs. Sam Davis, George S. Hughes, Mrs. E. H. Stiles, J. J. O'Dowd, N. A. Schell, J. H Huntsman, F.E.A. Kimball, Walter Lovejoy; Upper Sabino - F. H. Pauli, Mrs. Eleanor Nichols, Roy L. Bollin, H. H. Zellweger, O. J. Baughn, W. M. Killen, and B. F. Wilcox and Carter Canyon - Judge William H. Sawtelle, S. L. Kingan, H. A. Morrison, A. W. Olcott, and C. R. Lehman. In addition, there were thirty cottages on private land in Summerhaven. In the same year, several hundred campers were expected to use free campgrounds which now had running water and sanitary facilities.[126]

In May 1921 a major forest fire threatened homes in Summerhaven. The fire burned more than 10,000 acres and was fought by hundreds of local townspeople as well as the Forest Service. A hundred University of Arizona students joined Tucsonans, some of whom closed their businesses to go fight the fire. Local women went to the mountains to cook for the firefighters. The Forest Service was severely criticized for failing to act quickly with enough resources and for allowing the fire to get out of hand.[127] Planes were used for the first time as part of the fire control effort. The fire burned from the Canada del Oro area to what is now the ski lift area and then down Alder Canyon.

A Nature School was opened in the summer of 1930 in Summerhaven by Lydia B. Ransier for children between the ages of 6 and 15. The camp was started to provide care for children when their parents were on vacation. Ms. Ransier reported that the campers were "happy, gained weight, and were enthusiastic over their nature collections[128]

Chapter 11

THE HITCHCOCK HIGHWAY

It was just a matter of time before the issue of a better, shorter road up the mountain surfaced again. The people who owned cabins wanted better access. Entrepreneurs, who were dreaming of a full fledged winter resort with ski and bobsled runs, toboggan slides and ice rinks, wanted an improved road to bring up more visitors. State Legislator F. E. A. Kimball described the new road as an economic necessity:

> No better investment could be made by Tucson as a new road would save in a few years the cost of construction. The trip could be made in an hour and a half instead of taking three hours and a half as at present. The saving made in cost of gasoline and depreciation of cars is certainly no small item...Tucson now pays upwards of fifty thousand dollars a year for its wood. A road up this side of the mountain would render available each season at least the cost of half that amount, now going to waste. The road would also result in a marvelous saving of money now expended outside of Arizona by Tucson residents, as the new road would cause thousands of local

people to spend their vacations in the Catalinas where they now go east or to California...The cost of building a road up Sabino Canyon is assured when the people of Tucson desire it to become a reality...As we now have a first class road to Sabino Canyon, the remainder of the road to Soldier's Camp would be only 15.9 miles. This road would be less than one half the length of the present road from Tucson and unsurpassed by any road in the world for beauty of natural scenery.[129]

His argument almost made the road construction sound both necessary and easy and it began a local crusade for the new road.[130]

Debate raged among Tucsonans about the proposed highway. Opponents said that the cost would be enormous and that less than 2% of the population visited the Catalinas. Proponents said that many more people could enjoy these mountains if there were a better road. Opponents said that there was not enough water in the mountains to support more intensive usage, while proponents said that there was plenty of water and that any water shortages were due to inefficient piping and undeveloped springs.[131]

In 1930, the Santa Catalina Highway headquarters was set up in downtown Tucson. A survey of the new road was undertaken in 1931 by the U. S. Forest Service, the State Highway Commission, and the United States Bureau of Roads. The short route through Sabino Canyon, originally suggested by Kimball, proved too steep, and the final plan included a longer route through Molina Basin and Bear Canyon which required no tunnels. The debate about the new road finally ended when construction began in 1933.

One of the main reasons that the road got built was the untiring support of former Postmaster General Frank Hitchcock, who had also been an editor and publisher of the <u>Tucson Daily Citizen</u>. Hitchcock was a Harvard-educated lawyer who had an uncanny knack for getting things done. During his stint as Postmaster General, he introduced the ideas of postal savings, parcel post and airmail. Hitchcock had enough clout with the federal government to get the $1.25 million appropriated to start the road. Hitchcock proposed using federal prisoner labor to help construct the road, thereby reducing the costs considerably. At the time, many federal prisons were crowded with bootleggers, creating a need for more prisons or some other way of caring for the prisoners. Hitchcock convinced the Federal Government that the Catalinas were a perfect site for using prison labor since the climate was healthful and the area was isolated yet near a population center for supplies and services. Hitchcock's idea was readily approved by President Hoover, who signed the order providing establishment of the prison camp to build the highway.[132] For many years after its completion, the road was called the Hitchcock Highway, and one of the campgrounds in Bear Canyon is still called General Hitchcock.

The prison camp to accommodate the workers was first set up in tents near the top of the mountain near the present-day Boy Scout Camp, but cold weather and an invasion of skunks caused the camp to be relocated on the desert floor near the mouth of Soldier Canyon.[133] Although the prisoners lived in tents, the camp had a large mess hall with a kitchen and a baseball field which was the site of several games between the prisoners and members of a nearby CCC camp. The prison camp had minimum security, with no locked doors or gun-carrying guards. The prison wall was a line of whitewashed rocks laid in the hills around the camp. During the many years of prison operation, there were a few escapes attempts but none were successful. Most of the inmates were illegal aliens from Mexico and bootleggers, but there were also a few murderers and tax evaders.

RAILROAD CARS WERE USED IN BUILDING THE CATALINA HIGHWAY--HITCHCOCK NICKNAMED THE OPERATION THE CATALINA SHORT LINE. (Courtesy of the Coronado National Forest, Tucson, Arizona)

LAYING A CULVERT AT CATNIP CANYON (MILEPOST 8.8). (Courtesy of the Coronado National Forest, Tucson, Arizona)

After six years of work, the prison camp was moved six miles up the new road to Vail Corral near Molina Basin. The new site needed a well which was "witched" by Ralph Augustus Wetmore using a forked branch from a mesquite tree. The spot he chose finally produced abundant water after 45 days of drilling through solid granite.[134]

At first, the prisoners were allowed to use only hand tools. Removal of rock and debris was done by a brigade of wheelbarrows; granite was drilled by hand for blasting. Timber was cleared and the wood used to construct culverts. Unlike today, most of the natural vegetation that got in the way of the highway construction was simply destroyed. The prisoners became discouraged with their limited equipment, and after a few months, the federal government supplied them with air drilling equipment and dump trucks which made the grueling work somewhat less difficult. Driving the dump truck was a coveted position and aspirants for these jobs tried out on the baseball field. Many of the illegal Mexican aliens were assigned to operate the jackhammers and became very skilled. Some reported that they were able to secure good jobs as jackhammer operators when they were later deported to Mexico. In addition to working on the roads, the prisoners also received vocational training in mechanical drawing, gas and electric welding and machine shop.[135]

The camp was lucky to have a very skilled scrounger. Major pieces of equipment used to build the road, including hundreds of feet of light railway track, several mining cars, a bulldozer and a cement mixer, were acquired mysteriously "without exchange of funds."[136]

In February 1939 the prisoners and staff were moved to a permanent facility at Vail Corral in Molina Basin between Milepost 7 and 8. Amenities there included several barracks, a mess hall with kitchen, laundry and power houses, and a small sawmill. At its peak, this facility housed nearly 300 prisoners and staff members.

World War II provided the camp with additional labor from draft dodgers and conscientious objectors. At this same time, hardened criminals from the Terminal Island Penitentiary in San Diego were also brought to the camp when that prison was turned over to the Navy. The latter prisoners created anxiety among the camp officials, primarily because of a powder magazine that was part of the camp and was used in the road construction. To safeguard the explosives, they turned to the aid of one of the prisoners who happened to be one of the nation's top safecrackers. The prisoner designed a failsafe combination lock for the magazine.[137]

In 1943 Air Force engineers used parts of the road that had been completed for training activities. Some of the prisoners who were CO's went on a sit down strike, protesting that their work on the road was being used to help the war effort. The strike was ended quickly.

In 1943 and again in 1945, the Forest Service hired the prisoners for 35 cents per day to help fight forest fires. They fought fires not only in the Catalinas but in other Arizona forests as well. The prisoners welcomed the opportunity to earn some money, but their absence did slow work on the highway.

All prisoners sent to the Catalina highway site were supposed to be physically fit and capable of hard work. The few who were not were used to clean and cook for the camp. Vegetables for the camp were grown on ten acres of irrigated land in the Tanque Verde valley which had been leased by the Prison Bureau. The Bureau also sent some of the inmates to New Mexico to pick beans and dig potatoes to help feed the camp.[138]

By 1940, the road was completed as far as the prison camp. The prisoners kept on blasting, clearing and grading at the rate of a little less than two miles a year. By 1946, the road was paved to Soldier Camp. It was expected to reach Summerhaven the next year, but a cold winter caused some of the road to break and a portion had to be repaved, delaying the completion.

As soon as a piece of the road was finished, picnickers used the recreation areas that were created. Parking places were built at the most scenic locations, and boulder barricades were placed at the edges of the most hazardous portions of the road. Rock formations and other scenic phenomena found alongside the new road were given names and marked with "rustic signs." As many as 2000 people used the unfinished highway every weekend in the summer, to see the newly developed sights. Over 30,000 Tucson and Phoenix residents visited the Catalinas on Labor Day in 1947.

Paving was completed in 1949. The center stripe was drawn in a unique manner. A hole was drilled behind the driver's seat in a sedan, and a fine line of paint dripped out onto the highway as the driver went up and then back down the mountain. The center stripe was placed exactly in the center of these two lines. The road was completed in 1950, although work on side roads continued for several more months. Hitchcock did not live to see the finished product, as he had died in 1937. Nearly 8,000 prisoners had toiled for almost 18 years to construct the road, in contrast to the three years of work required to build the dirt road up the back side. The prison camp eventually became a federal youth detention center. The residents, who were known as the Hilltoppers, engaged in a number of projects, including maintaining campgrounds and fighting fires.

When the new road was first planned, it was assumed that the paving would continue over the top and down the old road on the back side, but there seemed to be little enthusiasm for this idea in 1950. The new highway had cost the federal government over a million dollars and had reduced the time for visitors to get to the summit to one hour. On March 10, 1951, the federal government turned over the road to Pima County for maintenance. Claude Hillman. Superintendent of Construction for the project, concluded his final report with this prophecy:

> The Catalina Mountains will no longer resound with heavy explosives and the clattering of jackhammers on the granite slopes, but there is a new undertone, that of racing motors ascending the mountain, which will increase in volume as time goes on.[139]

Some of the first people to drive up the new road were terrified by its twists and turns and sheer precipices. Many drivers today have the same reaction and the 25 miles of the Catalina Highway is considered the most dangerous road in Pima County. In spite of its possible perils, over a million trips are made up the highway each year.

During those eighteen years while the road was being built, life at the top went on much as it had since 1920, when the back road was completed. People who owned cabins then remember that life seemed much simpler. Cabins were left unlocked and there was a sense of camaraderie between the cabin owners and the Forest Service rangers. Without electricity, perishables were kept fresh by storage in the streams. It wasn't uncommon to see watermelons stuffed among the rocks in the creek. Washing was done on scrub boards while cooking was done on woodstoves and reading at night was aided by Coleman lanterns. On Saturday night, there was usually a Western band at the lodge. Everyone would get a little drunk, and occasionally fights would break out.

Forest Service employee John Brinkley and his wife Gerry lived at Palisades. She recalls that until the early 1950's there were only about three families who wintered over on the mountain. John Brinkley was famous for his ability to find lost hikers in the mountains, with the assistance of his faithful horse, Lucky. He knew the mountains so well that he seemed to be able to guess where the errant hikers probably went wrong and where they would end up.[140]

New Yorkers Randolph "Pat" and Julia Jenks, who first came to Mt. Lemmon in 1938, wintered in the Catalina foothills, but spent every summer on Mt. Lemmon for many years. As soon as the weather would begin to get hot, Ms. Jenks would take their goat, food, household supplies and their nanny up the back side in their Chevy coupe. Mr. Jenks would take the children up the front trail on horseback. They would return to Tucson once a month for more supplies. Although the family goat went up and down the mountain with the family, their chickens were left on the mountain to fend for themselves in the winter. The Jenks claimed their chickens mated with the wild turkeys and produced mixed offspring which they called "chiturks." They admitted they had never heard of this happening to anyone else on the mountain. The Jenks adopted a fawn which they named Bambi, who became a household pet. Bambi was taken down the mountain to reside with them in their winter home, where he laid in front of the fireplace, played with their dog and dined on graham crackers. But Bambi also ate flowers, and a disgruntled neighbor whose garden had been well chewed hauled the deer back up to Mt. Lemmon. Years later, the Jenks family saw a beautiful buck in the Catalinas who they thought was Bambi but they had no graham crackers to offer him so they could never be sure.[141]

During the 1930's, The Civilian Conservation Corps (CCC) developed the Sabino Canyon Recreation Area. They built roads, nine bridges and the one-and-one-half acre Sabino Lake. A much larger lake had originally been proposed, but the idea was scrapped due to inadequate funding and local squabbles.

FISHING ON THE SPILLWAY AT SABINO LAKE, LOCATED IN LOWER SABINO CANYON, PROBABLY IN THE 1940'S. (Courtesy of the Arizona Historical Society, Tucson, Arizona, #7239)

Sabino Lake did provide fishing for nearly two decades, but had problems with silt and leaf mold which could not be cured. After many attempts at dredging, maintenance of the lake for fishing ceased although the silt that was dredged was used to enrich gardens throughout Tucson. The lake serves as a birdwatching spot today.

The CCC also constructed wooden picnic tables; however, these were burned for firewood by picnickers within three months and were replaced by concrete ones. Even back then, Sabino Canyon was a great place for parties. In 1935, one Tucsonan complained in a letter to the editor of the Arizona Daily Star that it was not uncommon to see "couples taking advantage of the seclusion of the canyon" and that heavy drinking was the "order of the day." The letter writer was most upset by the number of nude bathers in the Canyon.[142]

The Summerhaven Land and Improvement District continued to own most of the private land until the late 1930's when "Pat" Jenks, bought them out. Jenks also owned a large mining claim, which he subdivided and sold as lots. Although this type of land acquisition was later made illegal, this deal resulted in an increase of private land in the Catalinas from 160 acres to its present day size of over 200 acres.

Chapter Twelve

SUMMERHAVEN GROWS UP

One of the men who would help shape the modern development of Summerhaven first visited the Catalinas in 1937 on a deer hunting trip. Tony Zimmerman would later recall that the drive up the mountain had made him sick, but that he "fell in love with her" anyway. In spite of his fulltime teaching job in Tucson, Zimmerman started buying property and selling real estate for Jenks. He eventually owned 60 acres of private land. He and his wife, Sena, bought the Mt. Lemmon Store in 1942. A year later, Zimmerman quit his teaching job, moved his family to Summerhaven and purchased the old Mariposa Lodge, which was then called the Mt. Lemmon Lodge. He especially loved those early years when he could roam the mountains all day and sometimes not see another soul. He could enjoy the coyotes howling behind his lodge on snowy days, as well as abundant coatimundi, turkeys, deer and trout. He delighted in the beavers in the streams but was dismayed when they were hunted down by some of the soldiers stationed at the radar station in the early 1950's. In all his years in the Catalinas, he saw only one rattlesnake and that was on the north slope.

THE MT. LEMMON LODGE WAS BUILT IN THE EARLY 1920'S BY THE
WESTFALLS--IT BURNED IN 1970. (Courtesy of the Arizona Historical
Society, Tucson, Arizona, #76189)

THE PINE CONE ROOM PICTURED IN AN AD FOR THE MT. LEMMON
LODGE, 1948. (Courtesy of the Arizona Historical Society, Tucson, Arizona)

In 1945, Zimmerman sold the Mt. Lemmon Lodge and bought the Neoli Lodge which was located at the mouth of Carter Canyon. He renamed it the Pinetree Lodge. Unfortunately, the Pinetree and the beautiful trees surrounding it burned down in 1950. Zimmerman suspected that the fire may have been caused by a disgruntled employee but he could never prove it.

In the same year he operated the Mt. Lemmon Sawmill which stood where the Post Office stands today. Zimmerman recalls that the old sawmill, which had been operating in the 1920's, had been abandoned by the time Zimmerman bought it and nearly all of the equipment stolen. He later moved the sawmill to its current site on Oracle Ridge. This sawmill burned down too. The night it burned down over a hundred University of Arizona students had enjoyed a party in the area and Zimmerman suspected that they had somehow caused the fire.

At one time, Zimmerman sold lumber for movie sets to Old Tucson. He even worked with some movie moguls who were interested in building a huge stone hotel with ski lodge, tennis courts, stables and narrow gauge railroad in Summerhaven. He said later he was glad that deal fell through.

One of Zimmerman's most significant accomplishments was the formation of the water cooperative. When he first started spending time in the Catalinas, he could see that most cabins were built near streams and that eventually the water supply would limit future development. In 1940 he called a meeting of cabin owners and organized a nonprofit water organization. Fortunately, Randolph Jenks, who owned hundreds of lots at the time, donated all of his rights in the springs to the water co-op. That allowed the co-op members to focus on two other critical problems--the storage of water and its distribution. Zimmerman was involved in procuring and placing several water tanks near Summerhaven. One was made of 3.5" redwood staves and the others were metal. Pipeline was laid from the springs to the tanks to create a reliable water supply all year. This nonprofit group, now called the Mt. Lemmon Water Cooperative, continues to serve many of the cabins in the area today.

Perhaps the project that was Zimmerman's greatest joy was the building and operating of the Mt. Lemmon Inn. This two story building in the heart of Summerhaven had 12 sleeping rooms, a dance hall, a restaurant, a bar, a country store and two gas pumps. Its foundation is visible today just north of the Alpine Inn. Zimmerman did some of the cooking himself and was famous for his hotcakes. He remembers cooking hotcakes one morning for 60 firefighters who had worked all night trying to control a fire. One of the men was Carl Sollers, an official with the Forest Service, who said he was hungry enough to eat two dozen by himself. Tony counted as Sollers ate twenty four hotcakes. (Sollers died tragically several years later in an air crash in the line of duty. A helicopter pad and road in the Catalinas are named for him.) Zimmerman sold the lodge in 1961 and got it back in 1968. It, too, burned to its stone foundation, in 1977.

In his early days in the mountains, Zimmerman served as a volunteer postmaster, distributing mail out of his store. In the 1950's, he and his wife had a bus franchise and drove a fifteen passenger bus on daily trips to Tucson to deliver passengers and mail. He recalls that one year there was a bad rock slide at Bear Canyon and the road was closed for a week. Since the mail had to be delivered, he and his wife worked out a system. She brought the mail from Tucson to the site of the slide, where he met her and took the mail on up to Summerhaven.

In 1948 Zimmerman was responsible for inviting up one of Summerhaven's more famous visitors. Zimmerman knew that presidential candidate Thomas Dewey was staying at the old El Conquistador Hotel in Tucson, so he left a message inviting him to see Mt. Lemmon. The next day, two limousines with several passengers, including Dewey, arrived at his lodge and spent a couple of hours enjoying the scenery.[143]

One of Mt. Lemmon's more colorful characters was a man who worked for Zimmerman. In the early 1940's, Buster Bailey leased an old homestead in what is now Catalina State Park, from where he guided winter visitors on horseback rides into Montrose and Romero Canyons. After serving in World War II, he came to Mt. Lemmon where he met Zimmerman, who hired him to do all sorts of jobs including running the mail. Bailey also played the mouth harp in a little band that played for Saturday night dances at the Inn.

Mares were Bailey's true love, and he had plenty during his years in the Catalinas. He says that one of his favorite horses, Baby, liked to go into the old Mt. Lemmon Inn and drink 7-Up and he had a picture to prove it, although the photo cannot be located today. Tony Zimmerman recalls that Baby "you know what" in the bar and a scoop shovel was brought in to clean up the mess. Bailey loved all the mountain's creatures except for one--the mountain lion--because of what a lion could do to a horse. His one regret is that he did not continue a small business he had started in the late 1930's taking people on tours of several caves in Peppersauce Canyon. He quit the business when too many people found out about the caves and began to tear them up.[144]

The completion of the highway brought a surge in the demand for new homes and inevitably increased the use of the mountains. In 1948 the Mt. Lemmon Realty Company, owned and operated by Tony Zimmerman, was selling many lots due to the tremendous public demand. The demand for leased land far exceeded the supply and the Forest Service responded by making more land available. Loma Linda, a new development of sixty-five homesites, was opened in the fall of 1948.[145] The number of cabin sites at Soldier Camp and Willow Canyon was greatly expanded. Annual rents for leased lots ranged from $25 to $45. New rental cabins were added to accommodate the mountain visitors.

At midcentury, the Forest Service eagerly supported the development of the mountains. In 1948, the Supervisor of the Coronado National Forest, C. A. Merker, discussed their plans, which included "complete facilities for homes; summer and winter resorts with lodges, inns and shops; ski areas; picnic and camping areas, etc--all under permit on National Forest land."[146]

The Forest Service was busily building more recreation sites to accommodate the expected influx of visitors due to the new road. By 1948, many projects were being worked on simultaneously. In Molina Basin, several picnic sites and a horse corral were made ready. Rose Canyon could be used as a temporary recreation site (although there was no lake there then). Soldier Camp had eight units and water. Inspiration Rock had facilities for fifty people, but no water, and Upper Sabino and Marshal Gulch had forty units with water and fireplaces.[147]

At about the same time the Hitchcock Highway was completed, electricity was brought to the settlements at the top of the mountains. Until that time, cabin owners had gone without electricity or had their own generators. The Mt. Lemmon Inn showed movies with a projector powered by a gasoline motor. The viewers had frequent unexpected intermissions when the motor ran out of gas. The Inn went through two motors before the Trico power company brought a power line to Summerhaven in 1950. The line stretched from Oracle Road to Summerhaven over a rough route through Cargodera Canyon. During the clearing of the path for the power line, numerous mishaps occurred, including the loss of horses to overexertion and the destruction of an Army half track truck.[148]

96

Perhaps the only natural feature lacking in the Catalinas was a good fishing lake. Soldier Lake, after all, was really the size a pond and Sabino Lake was always plagued with silt problems. In 1951, plans were begun for a much larger lake in the Rose Canyon area. Construction began in 1954 using labor from the federal prison site. Funds came from the Arizona Game and Fish Department, the U.S. Forest Service and Pima County Parks and Recreation. The project cost $79,000. Two dams were built to contain an eight acre lake. The lower dam was 45 feet from the stream bed to its top and 37 feet thick at its base. After the construction was finished, problems developed with leaks in the dams and acid in the water, which delayed the opening of the lake for fishing until 1960.[149]

The one man-made attraction that was lacking was a ski area. One of the early skiers in the Catalinas was Lowell Thomas, the news commentator, who came to these mountains when he was in Tucson visiting his son who was stationed at Davis Monthan Air Force Base. The two Thomases and three other men explored the mountains in the winter of 1944 looking for an ideal ski area. With the help of the forest rangers, they cleared an area at Bear Wallow for a quarter mile ski run and set up a rope tow using a Model T Ford motor. The association of the five men eventually evolved into the Sahuaro Ski Club, Tucson's first ski club. One of the original founders went on to become an Olympic skier.

By the late 1940's, the Forest Service had developed plans to build a larger ski facility in the area above Summerhaven. In 1953 federal prison labor was used to build the road up to the site of what is now Mt. Lemmon Ski Valley. The prisoners also helped clear ski runs and build the ski lodge. By the next year, there was a 1,000 foot run and a tow line 580 feet long. All of a sudden, business at Summerhaven could be as good on a winter day as during the summer as Tucsonans flocked to see the southernmost ski area in the U. S.. The ski lodge used timbers supplied by Tony Zimmerman. The site was designated as an official ski area in 1957. In 1964 a poma lift was added which was later replaced by a chair lift.[150]

For many decades, the children who were permanent residents on Mt. Lemmon had to be bussed down to Tucson schools. Their two-and-a-half-hour commute considerably lengthened their school day beyond that of most Tucson children. In 1953, the Pima County School Superintendent agreed that Mt. Lemmon needed its own school. The school was first housed in a private cabin and was moved twice in the next several years. By 1962, the need for a permanent sight was recognized. A cabin at the school's present site was purchased, and a partition was removed from between the former living room and bedroom, and playground equipment was purchased. Many improvements were made over the next few years, including building a home for the teacher. In 1974, the name of the school was changed to the Zimmerman Accommodation School, in honor of Tony Zimmerman.

Mother Nature asserted herself in the winter of 1967 with a snowstorm that created twenty foot drifts. The residents on the mountain were stranded for two weeks. Several moved into the Ponderosa Lodge, where mattresses were placed around the fireplace. Food and supplies were airlifted in. The only way the hotel "guests" could see outside was to climb on the roof.

In the late 1960's, Summerhaven was sometimes called "Hippie Haven," as its beauty and simple lifestyle attracted many young folks, some of whom thought that the mountains had special healing powers. A common practice among some was to stay in cabins during the week, undetected by the owners who usually came on the weekends. Some believed that the Catalinas were a natural landing spot for flying saucers and that a "Book of Life" was buried somewhere in the mountains.

Gerard Kuiper, a renowned astronomer who pioneered many fields in stellar and solar system research, helped bring telescopes to the Catalinas. Kuiper moved to Tucson in 1960 to work at the University of Arizona where he set up the Lunar and Planetary Laboratory. In his search for the best sites for observatories, he flew over nearby mountain ranges and selected the Catalinas because of the calm and dry air, relatively infrequent cloud cover, proximity to the campus and accessibility during winter snows. He estimated that astronomers in the Catalinas could observe the heavens on two out of every three nights.

In 1962, Kuiper located the first Catalina observatory site on Mt. Bigelow near where a Mountain States Telephone installation was being vacated. The dome was constructed in 1963 during heavy snows and housed a 21" reflecting telescope. Two years later, a 61-inch precision optical reflector scope was also installed. In addition to the building and dome for the scope, a ten room dormitory with a "tunnel" to the observatory was built for access during heavy snows. The 61-inch telescope was Kuiper's "pride and joy" and he made frequent visits to the site during its installation.[151] This telescope was used in the late 1960's to help map the lunar surface for the Apollo moon landing. This large scope is still found on Mt. Bigelow along with a 16-inch Schmidt which is used whenever a wide field of vision is required such as observing comets. Television transmitters for Channels 4, 9, and 13 are located beyond the telescopes at the very top of Mt. Bigelow.

In 1970, the U. S. Air Defense Command abandonned its radar station at the summit of Mt. Lemmon. The University of Arizona Lunar and Planetary Laboratory leased the site from the U. S. Forest Service. The operation was ideal for infrared observations which require both high altitude and dry air. In fact, Kuiper believed that Mt. Lemmon was the highest and driest mountain top in the U. S. that was accessible on a year

MAIN OBSERVATORY SITE AT SUMMIT OF MT. LEMMON IN 1970'S.
(Courtesy of the Lunar and Planetary Laboratory, University of Arizona)

round basis. By the mid 1970's, a machine shop, powerhouse, water supply and dormitories had been added.[152] The 20 acre area on the summit was not used exclusively by the University of Arizona. The forest service housed firefighters in a dorm there and other universities installed domes and telescopes. At the present time, facilities at Mt. Lemmon are used by the University of Arizona, the University of Minnesota, and Ft. Huachuca. Microwave communications equipment is also located in the area. The Catalina observatories, along with other major operations at Kitt Peak and Mt. Hopkins, help make Tucson a major center for astronomy.

Chapter Thirteen

PRECARIOUS PARADISE

The optimism of the people of the 1950's regarding the ability of the mountain to withstand development seems astonishing today. Many of the people who then lived in Summerhaven seemed to think that several lakes and ski areas and a highway down the north side of the mountain to Oracle would be the best thing that could happen. Many believed development could not, and should not, be stopped. Visitors seemed content to see movies at the Mt. Lemmon Inn, bowl at the radar station and rent horses from the two stables, all without much concern for the future. The Forest Service joined in this optimism and was making plans to open a second ski area in the Bear Wallow area.

By the 1970's and 1980's, however, perspectives began to change. The effect of greater usage and development on the environment became a grave concern. A 1972 feature article in the Arizona Daily Star drew a bleak picture of Summerhaven, describing the sewage problems, untidy buildings, burned remnants of a lodge, polluted streams and roving dog packs.[153] These land use problems created great turmoil among the Forest

Service staff, the cabin owners, Pima County government and many environmental groups. The first sewer line, installed in the 1950's, was washed out by a flood in 1978, and sewage contaminated the creeks. Pima County officials, the Forest Service and the residents argued about what to do to fix the problem.

The momentum of development began to slow as parts of the mountains were returned to less intense uses. The old prison camp, which had been converted into a facility for juvenile offenders and later an Indian youth center, was razed in 1973.[154] In 1978, the roads in Sabino Canyon, that had been so proudly built in the 1930's, were closed and replaced by a tram that shuttled visitors up and down the canyon. In the late 1970's, a large area of land bordering the Catalinas to the west, which had been a home of the Hohokam, was saved from a housing development and turned into Catalina State Park. In 1978, the Pusch Ridge Wilderness area was established.

In the 1970's, some leases on forest service lands in other parts of the Coronado National Forest were not renewed, and cabin owners were forced to tear down their cabins and restore the land to its original condition. Cabin owners on leased land in the Catalinas began to fear that they might not be allowed to stay indefinitely and that cabins which had been lovingly crafted decades ago might be razed. In the late 1980's, an effort was launched to save leased cabins by trying to persuade the Forest Service to sell some of the leased land to the leaseholders, with the assurance that no new development will occur in the privatized areas.

In 1982 Pima County built a sewage treatment plant between Marshall Gulch and Summerhaven to help reduce the pollution of Sabino Creek. County building codes were made increasingly tough so that new building became difficult and costly, if not impossible, on many private parcels. A few years later, Tucson Clean and Beautiful, with the assistance of helicopter crews from the U. S. Marines, took on the project of cleaning up 43 wrecked vehicles which littered the canyons below the Catalina Highway.

A long range road renovation project was started in 1988 to tame the Catalina Highway by creating a wider, safer road by the end of the century. In contrast to building practices during the original Catalina Highway construction, new policies require that all natural vegetation be saved wherever possible and shoulders are relandscaped as soon as a stretch of the new highway is finished. A new roadside observation and rest stop was created at milepost 3 called Babat Duag--the Tohono O'odham name for the Catalinas.

The development of Biosphere II begun in the late 1980's and located in the northern foothills west of Oracle has brought international attention to this area for the first time. This experimental glass enclosed structure may someday serve as a prototype for self sustaining space colonies. The sphere's residents will have a magnificent view of the Catalinas as they conduct experiments which will help scientists better understand the earth's environment and may ultimately allow humans to live permanently in outer space.

The Catalinas continue to draw visitors with their "still and solemn mystery". More than one million trips are made up the Catalina Highway each year according to some estimates. Not all visitors make it all the way to the top, however, but stop somewhere along the way to enjoy any of 17 recreation sites with more than 560 picnic and camping units. Many stop at Windy Point to take pictures of the valley while others opt for a quiet day of fishing at Rose Canyon. In the winter, the roads to Rose Canyon and Mt. Bigelow are popular areas for cross country skiing. The chair lift at Mt. Lemmon Ski Valley may have a long line when the snow is good and the Catalina

Highway is open, a combination that does not happen as often as many would like. Many find solitude hiking on the 40+ maintained trails--even on a summer holiday weekend most of the trails are not crowded. Other visitors delight in the hunting opportunities during the seasons for quail, deer and javelina.

In the Summerhaven and Soldier Camp areas, there are nearly 600 cabins on leased and private land including those owned by the 50-70 year round residents. Three restaurants, two gift shops, a new mercantile, cabin rentals and a lodge provide services to many visitors. Sunday services are held regularly at the Community Church and educational programs are occasionally scheduled in the summer at the new fire station.

By the 1990's, the century long effort of finding better ways to get more people into the Catalinas quicker to engage in more diverse activities has definitely slowed to a crawl. One hundred years of development has indeed resulted in some environmental changes, but the Catalinas are still incredibly beautiful--every season of the year. These mountains continue to provide an escape from city life for greenery-starved Tucsonans as well as a home for year round residents. People who visit the Catalinas for the first time now may not lament or even notice the damage that has been done, but simply appreciate the beauty that remains. For many, this mountain range is a refuge, just as it was for the Apaches who ate its acorns and roamed its slopes and gazed out onto the desert below. In spite of the wounds, the Catalinas are still the paradise that has drawn people here for centuries.

ENDNOTES

1. Jeffrey F. Burton, Prehistoric Rock Art of the Southeastern Arizona Uplands: A Formal Record of Fifty Three Rock Art Sites on the Coronado National Forest, (Tucson, Arizona: Coronado National Forest, July, 1988), pp. 186-254.

2. Grenville Goodwin, Social Organization of the Western Apache, (Chicago: University of Chicago Press, 1942), p. 4.

3. Burton, pp. 232 and 291.

4. Anne E. Harrison, "The Santa Catalinas: A Description and History," Sabino Canyon Visitor's Center Manuscript, 1969, pp.73, 80-81, 131 and 136.

5. Goodwin, p. 28.

6. C. L. Sonnichsen, Tucson: The Life and Times of an American City, (Norman, Oklahoma: University of Oklahoma Press, 1982) pp. 11-12.

7. Dobyns, Henry F., Spanish Colonial Tucson: A Demographic History, (Tucson, Arizona: University of Arizona Press, 1976), pp. 68 and 83.

8. Henry P. Walker, "Wagon Freighting in Arizona," The Smoke Signal (Fall, 1973), 181.

9. Henry Winfred Splitter (ed.), "Tour in Arizona: Footprints of an Army Officer by 'Sabre'", The Journal of the West, (July , 1962), p. 81.

10. Dan L. Thrapp, The Conquest of Apacheria, (Norman, Oklahoma: University of Oklahoma Press, 1967), pp. 160-161.

11. Arizona Weekly Star, June 9, 1887.

12. Arizona Weekly Star, June 16, 1887.

13. Post Return, Fort Lowell Record of Events, April 30, 1888.

14. Arizona Daily Star, June 5, 1890.

15. Catalina Savings and Loan,"Catalina View," 1978.

16. Issac Goldberg, Manuscript, 1894, Arizona Historical Society.

17. Arizona Weekly Star, July 28, 1881.

18. "Reminiscences of Alexander McKay as told to Mrs. George Kitt, Manuscript, Arizona Historical Society, n.d..

19. Harrison, pp. 85-86.

20. Elizabeth Lambert Wood, Arizona Hoof Trails (Portland, Oregon: Binfords and Mort, 1956), pp. 67-68.

21. George Stone Wilson, "Saga of Oracle, Mountain Cow Town," Arizona Cattlelog, (February, 1965), p. 58.

22. Arizona Weekly Star, August 18, 1881.

23. Harrison, p. 52; Wilson, p. 397; Arizona Daily Star, March 13, 1881.

24. Arizona Daily Star, June 8 and 19, 1892.

25. Wilson, p. 274.

26. Arizona Daily Star, March 1, 1970.

27. Harrison, p. 106.

28. "Reminiscences of Emerson Oliver Stratton as told to his daughter Edith Stratton," Manuscript, Arizona Historical Society.
See also Arizona Daily Star, June 22, 1919.

29. Wood, p 19.

30. Wood, p. 19; Harrison, p. 83; Arizona Weekly Star, August 18, 1881; Bernice Cosulich, Tucson, (Tucson, Arizona: Arizona Silhouettes, 1953), pp. 250-51.

31. Harrison, pp. 93-97.

32. Citizen, November , 1885.

33. Frank S. Crosswhite, "'J. G. Lemmon and Wife,' Plant Explorers in Arizona, California, and Nevada," Desert Plants, (August, 1979),pp. 18-19.

34. Mountain Echo, April 20, 1979.

35. Arizona Weekly Citizen, August 13, 1887.

36. Arizona Daily Star, May 4, 1887.

37. Arizona Daily Star, May 26, 1887.

38. Arizona Weekly Star, August 18, 1881.

39. Arizona Daily Star, October 16, 1896.

40. Arizona Daily Star, November 19, 1896.

41. Arizona Daily Star, April 7, 1897.

42. Will C. Barnes, Arizona Place Names, (Tucson, Arizona: Univeristy of Arizona Press), p. 260.

43. Harrison, p. 42.

44. Charles R. Ames, "A History of the Forest Service," The Smoke Signal, (Fall, 1967), p.122.

45. Arizona Daily Star, May 7, 1906.

46. Arizona Daily Star, July 3, 1906.

47. Arizona Daily Star, July 10 and July 22, 1906.

48. Arizona Daily Star, September 2, 1904.

49. Arizona Daily Star, September 2, 1904.

50. Arizona Daily Star, March 10, 1908.

51. Arizona Daily Star, September 16, 1908.

52. Harrison, p. 50.

53. Harrison, pp. 54, 156,

54. Ames, 1967, p. 142.

55. Harrison, p. 152.

56. Arizona Daily Star, October 5, 1911.

57. Arizona Daily Star, May 28, 1912.

58. Arizona Daily Star, June 22, 1919.

59. Arizona Daily Star, August 23, 1914.

60. Arizona Daily Star, April 18, 1917.

61. Harrison, p. 111.

62. Arizona Daily Star, March 15, 1917.

63. Harrison, pp. 90-192.

64. Arizona Daily Star, August 14, 1891.

65. Stratton manuscript.

66. Lowell Parker, Arizona Towns and Tales, (Phoenix, Arizona: Phoenix Newspapers, 1975), p. 269.

67. Arizona Daily Star, May 12, 1950.

68. Arizona Daily Star, February 24, 1939.

69. Elizabeth Lambert Wood, "A Sketch of the Life of Elizabeth Lambert Wood of Peppersauce Canyon, Oracle, Pinal County, Arizona," Manuscript, Arizona Historical Society.

70. Parker, p. 268.

71. DeWitt Harris Winget, Pipe Dreams: Stories of Buffalo Bill, (Clinton, Iowa, 1925).

72. Harrison, pp. 95-102.

73. Wilson, 1987, p. 349.

74. Tucson Citizen, August 3, 1958.

75. Parker, p. 271.

76. Wilson, April, 1965, p. 42.

77. Wilson, February, 1965, p. 56.

78. Parker, p. 270.

79. Tucson Citizen, April 27, 1928.

80. Harrison, pp. 69-70.

81. Arizona Daily Star, June 16, 1968.

82. Harrison, p. 52.

83. John P. Wilson, Islands in the Desert: A History of the Uplands of Southeast Arizona, (Las Cruces, New Mexico: National Forest Service, 1987), p. 398.

84. Harrison, p. 107.

85. Arizona Daily Star, March 1, 1970.

86. Edwin Knagge, Manuscript, Arizona Historical Society, 1982.

87. Mountain Echo, June 5, 1979.

88. Arizona Daily Star, March 25, 1962.

89. Arizona Daily Star, April 10, 1915; May 5, 1915; May 20, 1915.

90. Glenton G. Sykes, Manuscript, Arizona Historical Society.

91. Arizona Daily Star, August 24, 1920.

92. Arizona Daily Star, August 16, 1921.

93. Harrison, pp. 63-64.

94. Tucson Daily Citizen, April 13, 1969.

95. Harrison, p. 145.

96. Arizona Daily Star, November 13, 1910.

97. Harrison, p. 72.

98. Harrison, p. 72.

99. Harrison, pp. 51-52.

100. Harrison, pp. 138-39.

101. Arizona Daily Star, May 21, 1967.

102. Arizona Daily Star, March 1, 1970.

103. Arizona Daily Star, July 9, 1920.

104. Arizona Daily Star, May 21, 1967.

105. Tucson Citizen, May 14, 1928.

106. Harrison, p. 148.

107. Tucson Citizen, September 12, 1936.

108. Tucson Citizen, November 28, 1931.

109. Interview with Ted Knipe, 16 December 1990.

110. Mountain Echo, May 5, 1979.

111. Mountain Echo, July, 1979.

112. Arizona Daily Star, June 29, 1920

113. Arizona Daily Star, June 29, 1920.

114. Arizona Daily Star, July 9, 1920.

115. Arizona Daily Star, July 9, 1920.

116. Arizona Daily Star, July 28, 1920.

117. Arizona Daily Star, July 28, 1920.

118. Arizona Daily Star, July 28, 1920.

119. Arizona Daily Star, August 3, 1920.

120. Arizona Daily Star, July 20, 1920.

121. Wilson, February, 1965, p. 56.

122. Mountain Echo, March 20, 1979.

123. Mountain Echo, March, 1979.

124. Arizona Daily Star, July 30, 1916.

125. Harrison, p. 70.

126. Arizona Daily Star, February 12, 1923.

127. Citizen, May 2, 1923.

128. Tucson Daily Citizen, April 20, 1930.

129. Tucson Citizen, May, 1926.

130. Arizona Daily Star, February 28, 1928.

131. Tucson Citizen, November 11, 1928.

132. Arizona Daily Star, March 31, 1936.

133. Tucson Citizen, May 30, 1988.

134. Harrison, p. 91.

135. Arizona Daily Star, November 21, 1946.

136. Tucson Citizen, May 30, 1988.

137. Tucson Citizen, January 6, 1967.

138. Tucson Citizen, May 30, 1988.

139. Final Construction Report, Arizona Forest Highway Project 33, Catalina Highway, (Tucson, Arizona: U. S. Department of Commerce, Bureau of Public Roads, 1951) p. 122.

140. Charles Bowden, Frog Mountain Blues, (Tucson, Arizona: University of Arizona Press, 1987), pp. 82-83.

141. Mountain Echo, April 20, 1979.

142. Arizona Daily Star, February 20, 1935.

143. Tony Zimmerman, Manuscript, Arizona Historical Society; Bowden, pp. 86-91.

144. Mountain Echo, February 20, 1979.

145. "The Story of Mt. Lemmon," The Magazine Tucson (August, 1948), p. 24.

146. Ibid.

147. Harrison, pp. 66-67.

148. Harrison, pp. 49-50.

149. Arizona Daily Star, April 15, 1953; Tucson Citizen, December 25, 1954.

150. Arizona Daily Star, January 30, 1954; Mountain Echo, February 20, 1979.

151. Ewen Whitaker, The University of Arizona's Lunar and Planetary Laboratory: Its Founding and Early Years, (Tucson, Arizona: University of Arizona Printing Department, 1985) pp. 37-40.

152. Gerard P. Kuiper, "The Lunar and Planetary Laboratory and its Telescopes," Communications of the Lunar and Planetary Laboratory, (1972), pp. 222-225.

153. Arizona Daily Star, May 19, 1972.

154. Tucson Citizen, July 13, 1973.

SOURCES

NEWSPAPERS

Arizona Daily Star

Tucson Citizen

Mountain Echo (published on Mt. Lemmon in 1979 by Frances Morse)

PAMPHLETS

Catalina Savings and Loan, "Catalina View," 1978.

Lunar and Planetary Laboratory/University of Arizona, "Mt. Lemmon Observatory," 1976.

Oracle Centennial Celebration, "History of Oracle," May 26-28, 1973.

Summerhaven Land and Improvement Company, "Summerhaven: the Resort Incomparable", n.d.

JOURNAL AND MAGAZINE ARTICLES

Ames, Charles R. "A History of the Forest Service." The Smoke Signal, Fall, 1967, pp. 117-143.

Bowden, Charles. "The Santa Catalinas." Arizona Highways,   1986, pp. 32-35.

Crosswhite, Frank S. "J. G. Lemmon and Wife: Plant Explorers in Arizona, California and Nevada." Desert Plants, August, 1979, pp.12-19.

Cruikshank, Dale p. "20th-Century Astronomer." Sky and Telescope, March 1974, pp. 159-164.

Heald, Weldon F. "The Santa Catalinas." Arizona Highways, January 1965, pp.13-37.

Kuiper, Gerard P. "The Lunar and Planetary Laboratory and its Telescopes." Communications of the Lunar and Planetary Laboratory, University of Arizona, Communications No. 172, 1972, pp. 199-247.

"Oracle and the Colorful Story of the Mountain View Hotel." The Magazine Tucson, November, 1948, pp. 28-29.

Peterson, Thomas H. "Ft. Lowell, A. T. Army Post During the Apache Campaigns." The Smoke Signal, Fall, 1963, pp. 1-19.

Splitter, Henry Winfred (ed.). "Tour in Arizona: Footprints of an Army Officer by 'Sabre'." Journal of the West, July, 1962, pp. 74-97.

Steuer, Andrew. "The Santa Catalina Mountains: A Desert Sky Island." Desert, July 1981, pp. 8-13.

"The Story of Mt. Lemmon." The Magazine Tucson, August, 1948, pp. 18-25.

Vickers, Fred. "Mt. Lemmon--An All Year Resort." Progressive Arizona, June, 1926, pp.23-24.

Walker, Henry P. "Wagon Freighting in Arizona." The Smoke Signal, Fall, 1973, pp. 181-204.

GOVERNMENT BROCHURES AND DOCUMENTS

Burton, Jeffrey. Prehistoric Rock Art of the Southeastern Arizona Uplands: A Formal Record of Fifty Three Rock Sites on the Coronado National Forest. Tucson , Arizona: prepared for the Coronado National Forest Service; February, 1988.

U. S. Department of Commerce, Bureau of Public Roads, Division Seven. Final Construction Report, Arizona Forest Highway, Project 33 Catalina Highway. Tucson, Arizona: 1951.

U. S. National Forest Service, "Welcome to the Santa Catalina Ranger District of the Coronado National Forest," June, 1989.

U. S. National Forest Service, "History of the Santa Catalinas," June 1989.

Wilson, John P. Islands in the Desert: A History of the Uplands of Southeast Arizona. Las Cruces, New Mexico: contracted by the National Forest Service, 1987.

MANUSCRIPTS

Goldberg, Issac. "Santa Catalina Mountains." MS: Arizona Historical Society.

Kimball, F. E. A. "Biographical Sketch of a Worthy Pioneer." MS: Arizona Historical Society.

Knagge, Edwin. MS: Arizona Historical Society.

Harrison, Anne E. "The Santa Catalinas: A Description and History." Tucson, Arizona: Sabino Canyon Visitor's Center Manuscript, 1969.

McKay, Alexander. "Reminiscences of Alexander McKay as told to Mrs. George F. Kitt. MS: Arizona Historical Society.

Stratton, Emerson Oliver. "Reminiscences of Emerson Oliver Stratton as told to her daughter Edith Stratton." MS: Arizona Historical Society.

Sykes, Glenton G. "First Mt. Lemmon Road." MS. Arizona Historical Society.

Wood, Elizabeth Lambert. "A Sketch of the Life of Elizabeth Lambert Wood of Peppersauce Canyon, Oracle, Pinal County, Arizona." MS: Arizona Historical Society.

Zimmerman, Tony. MS: Arizona Historical Society.

INTERVIEWS

Cotten, Mary Childs. February 11, 1984.

Knipe, Ted. December 16, 1990.

Mortimer, Glenn. March 24, 1990.

Whitaker, Ewen. January 26, 1991.

Zimmerman, Tony. December 31, 1983.

BOOKS

Barnes, Will C. Arizona Place Names. Tucson, Arizona: University of Arizona Press, 1960.

Bowden, Charles. Frog Mountain Blues. Tucson, Arizona: University of Arizona Press, 1987.

Davis, Goode P. Jr.. Man and Wildlife in Arizona: The American Exploration Period 1824-1865. Phoenix, Arizona: Arizona Game and Fish Department, 1982.

Cosulich, Bernice. Tucson. Tucson, Arizona: Arizona Silhouettes, 1953.

Lockwood, Frank C. The Apache Indians. New York City, New York: The MacMillan Company, 1938.

McCarthy, Kieran. Desert Documentary. Tucson, Arizona: Arizona Historical Society Monograph, 1976.

Mails, Thomas. The People Called Apache. Englewood Cliffs, New Jersey: Prentice Hall, 1974.

Parker, Lowell. Arizona Towns and Tales. Phoenix ,Arizona: Phoenix Newspapers, 1975.

Schellie, Don. Vast Domain of Blood: The Story of the Camp Grant Massacre. Los Angeles, California: Westernlore Press, 1968.

Sonnichsen, C. L. Tucson: The Life and Times of an American City. Norman, Oklahoma: University of Oklahoma Press, 1982.

Thrapp, Dan L. The Conquest of the Apacheria. Norman, Oklahoma: University of Oklahoma Press, 1967.

114

Whitaker, Ewen. The University of Arizona's Lunar and Planetary Laboratory: Its Founding and Early Years. Tucson, Arizona: University of Arizona Printing Department, 1985.

Winget, DeWitt Harris. Pipe Dreams: Stories of Buffalo Bill. Clinton, Iowa, 1925.

Wood, Elizabeth Lambert. Arizona Hoof Trails. Portland, Oregon: Binfords and Mort, 1956.

For additional copies, please send
$8.95 per book plus 5% sales tax
plus $2.00 shipping and handling to:
Skunkworks Productions
P.O. BOX 672
Mt. Lemmon, Arizona 85619